CARDIFF AND THE SPANISH CIVIL WAR

Rob Stradling

Published by Butetown History & Arts Centre
5 Dock Chambers
Bute Street
Cardiff CF1 6AG

ISBN 1-898317-06-2 (Hardback)
ISBN 1-898317-07-0 (Paperback)

Acknowledgements
Sub-editors: Glenn Jordan, Chris Weedon
Editorial Assistance: Alan Milne
Production Manager: Marco Gil-Cervantes
Proofing: Ray Reed, Phyllis Chappell
Picture Research: Molly Maher
Indexing: Martin Hopkins

Design & typesetting: Word Up Design
Art reproduction & printing : AST Printing

This publication has been produced with
financial help from Cardiff County Council.

Butetown History & Arts Centre is supported by
Cardiff County Council, Cardiff Bay
Development Corporation and European
Regional Development Fund.

CAERDYDD CARDIFF
CYNGOR SIR CAERDYDD
CARDIFF COUNTY COUNCIL

CARDIFF BAY

List of Contents

1.
Edward Burra's painting 'Red Cloaked Figure', 1936.

2.
Mid-Glamorgan councillor Ray Davies examines damage to the Cathays Park International Brigade memorial following the vandal outrage of 1994.

Preface and Acknowledgements

In October, 1938, the International Brigades were stood down from the front in Catalonia. Following an emotional farewell parade in Barcelona, its members dispersed to their countries of origin. Among the Welsh contingent was Jim Brewer of Ebbw Vale, who had carried the standard of the British Battalion in the final march along the Rambla. Being greeted as a hero on return to his own radical working-class community was little surprise, but he was somewhat taken aback in Cardiff, where the veterans were entertained to dinner by the Publicity (Press) Club. 'There was a genuine sort of popular front feeling even around some of the Tories'[1], Brewer recalled many years later. At this function, he met an army officer who had recently - in the wake of the Munich crisis - been appointed to supervise the installation of air raid shelters in the city.

> He took me around the Cathays Park area where they had dug some preliminary shelters, and he was asking me what I thought, and I said 'this will save people's lives. Have one of these in every back garden to dive into ... I've been in much more open places than that and survived bombing', which reassured him.[1]

In this same vicinity today stands a memorial to the Welshmen who fought in the Spanish Civil War as members of the XV International Brigade. It is a simple block of granite, hewn into a monolith like those marking the sites of National Eisteddfodau. On two plaques it bears a celebrated phrase from the speech made by the Spanish communist politician, Dolores Ibárruri (known to the world as 'La Pasionaria') on the Barcelona occasion mentioned above, and a text from the writings of T.E. Jenkins, a notable Welsh (Christian) communist. On at least three occasions since its inauguration in November, 1992, this monument has been the object of attack by person or persons unknown, who have daubed it with crude insults and swastikas in red paint. The last of these assaults was particularly determined, the assailants setting fire to old tyres which they had stacked around the stone, and using heavy implements to prise off its metal inscriptions.

From whatever source these attacks originate, they indicate a strength of feeling, antipathetically connected to events and opinions enshrined in the memorial, which some may find sinister, others merely bizarre. This book records a lively exchange of views between opposed ex-combatants which took place in a local newspaper before the Spanish War had ended. During writing of the book, the correspondence columns of the local press once again demonstrated a difference of views, between one reader who felt the communist role in the Civil War was glorious and another who regarded it as being little less than shameful. Listen - if only for a moment - and you can hear reverberations of a bell that tolled in Spain sixty years ago.

My book attempts to explain why some minds still register an emotional response to a conflict distant from us in space and time, and which has no obvious relation to the city of Cardiff and to our present lives in it. To explain is not always to bring about understanding, but without explanation - however imperfect - understanding would never be possible. Research on the history of Cardiff, a home town which has deep significance for me, came as a by-product of a larger project dealing with Ireland's involvement in the Spanish Civil War. I have dim childhood memories of overhearing (perhaps underhearing would be better) arguments about Franco's Spain among grown-ups in our Grangetown home, amidst glasses of stout and sherry, and with a priest earnestly involved, at wedding parties or funeral obsequies. In recent years, a sequence of events acted together to return my mind to those far-off debates. First of all, I came across various documents in the archives of the Foreign Affairs Ministry in Madrid. One file concerned the long-forgotten affair of four Spanish merchant ships, marooned in the Docks in 1937; another, the despatch of a Francoist secret agent to spy on the Cardiff Spanish community; and yet another contained correspondence referring to P.O.W. José María Larreta, whose surname set another reverberation tintinabulating in my memory cells as I sat in the basement of what used to be the prison of the Spanish Habsburg Court, built during the reign of King Philip IV in the 1620s. These prompts, along with the approaching sixtieth anniversary of the Civil War, made me decide to expand what had been only a mental footnote into a detailed investigation.

The results have surprised and fascinated me - reactions which (naturally) I hope readers will share. In Jack Jones' so-called 'epic' novel *River out of Eden*, set in Cardiff in the century between 1848 and 1948, Owen Regan, heir of an Irish immigrant and self-made millionaire, becomes a close friend of the third marquis of Bute, and marries the daughter of a Barcelona businessman. She dies giving birth to a son, Tirso, whose daughter marries an Irishman (and so on). Despite all this 'duw, olé and begorrah!' stuff, the novelist was evidently ignorant of the events of the Spanish Civil War, for he has 'Sir Tirso' (Tirso Regan, Lord Pantmawr - if you please) going back to Barcelona for a holiday with his Spanish relatives in the year 1937, where in all probability he (and they) would have been shot on sight! In Tom Davies' more recent 'epic' novel *Fire in the Bay*, Tiger Bay's Somali secret society is weakened by the loss of its seamen members who take off for the Spanish War. All this is merely fiction; as usual in history, the reality is far more interesting, and in many respects more difficult to believe.

Of course, Cardiff is not the only British city which had connections with the Spanish Civil War. For example, the four ships mentioned above belonged to a fleet of thirty-five vessels, posing a problem in a dozen British ports, many of which also had residents of Spanish and Irish descent, and sent volunteers to the International Brigades. Yet I am convinced that no other city (except, perhaps, London) has such a richly complex story. In tracing it, I have tried to maintain proper objectivity. Whatever our personal reactions, we must keep in mind that people suffered equally on both sides in the tragedy of the Spanish Civil War, a consideration which applies through the whole spectrum of what can be classified as suffering. It could have been a matter of loss of earnings and the privation that goes with it; secret resentments against or public alienation from neighbours; homelessness and enforced exile from one's native land; long agony of mind, resulting from failure to follow a worthy ideal to the absolute limit demanded; being frightened and hungry, imprisoned in brutal circumstances, seriously wounded, or meeting with death in action, as a result of actually following those ideals. All these things, and others of equal moment, happened to both Spaniards and Cardiffians.

Although my shortest book, this one has by far the longest list of accessories before the fact. Joe Larreta must come first, not only as a reward for turning up so fortuitously in the archive, but also for his patient good humour in enduring a series of interviews which must have reminded him of his experiences of being 'grilled' as a prisoner-of-war. Luis Cicero, his wife Mary, daughter Carmen and brother-in-law Frank Sanchez, pooled their memories to feed me with rich material about both Spain itself and 'Spain-in-Cardiff'. I am additionally indebted to Carmen Ayres for drawing my attention to a press article about T.A.R. Hyndman, as I might otherwise have missed the whole Hyndman story. Very similar was the intervention of my friend and collaborator, Meirion Hughes, who spotted an important newspaper item about R.J. Peters. Information on 'the Latin Quarter' off James Street was provided by Doris and Pamela Perez, Vera Drakakis, and Norrie Russ; I have known these witnesses for most of my life, and the last-named has borne the added misfortune of being my second cousin. Cissie Davidson (née Conway) recalled - with typical droll humour - political attitudes among the Catholic working class in the 1930s. Dan O'Neill, once of Grangetown and now of *South Wales Echo* fame, smoothed my path into the Echo archive, and 'put me onto' a little-known incident in the career of Lord Haw-Haw. Frank Thomas generously allowed me to consult his memoirs of his service in Spain. Joyce Howells and Nancy Smith told me about Bill Coles; Chris Short, Paddy Kitson and Howard Williamson about the Tom Hyndman they knew in the 1970s. Among the stalwarts of the Butetown History and Arts Centre, Harry 'Shipmate' Cooke was a mine of information about the Cardiff docklands he adopted as a refugee scouser in the 1930s, and Allan Milne provided me with references derived from his ongoing work on the 'Cardiff Norwegians'. Alan Carter placed useful material about Penarth - and Fifi Roberts - at my disposal. Dannie Abse persistently replied to persistent harassments; whilst Dr. Stephens of Penarth alerted me to the history of another doctor-poet, Archie Cochrane. Pat Griffiths drew my attention to the life of Stanley Evans. Joan Evans gave me information about her late husband Ben. Nigel Gibbs sent details about his father, the late Mostyn, and Alun Emlyn-Jones performed a similar filial duty in respect of the late John Emlyn. Peter Francis trusted me with rare copies of *The Illtydian* magazine from the 1930s. I am grateful for the time and interest of all these, and others who contributed more inadvertently. For me, the sheer enjoyment of it all was a bonus.

I have also been lucky in having academic colleagues from every generation since the 1930s, who are guardians of personal memories and historical data. Christopher Hill was a legend in the History Department at Cardiff during my student days there, many years after he had left. I was glad to have the opportunity of talking to him about this book, an experience which (inevitably) resulted in the legend being corrected in several respects. It gives me delight to acknowledge the interest and help of my own tutor at the old University College, Evan Edwards, whose approaches to history and teaching have been a lasting influence. The writings of Professor Hywel Francis are closest in theme to the present one, and I have plundered them shamelessly. Much of my interest in the Basque Country has been due to the influence of my friend Miguel Angel Echevarría, Bilbaïno, European, and historian.

The British Library Newspaper Division at Colindale combined efficiency and friendly courtesy in coping with excessive demands on its resources. At the Miners' Library and the University Archive in Swansea, I was helped by Sian Williams, Jo Keenan and Elizabeth Bennet. In my own department, Geoff Boden and Ian Dennis collaborated on the production side. Finally (back at my other home) Celia and Helen were sources of information, argument, and practical assistance. I was happy that my son, Rob, found the history of contemporary Cardiff to be of greater interest than that of Habsburg Spain, and agreed to act as an unpaid (but reassuringly adept) research assistant in various aspects of the work. Finally, at the Butetown History & Arts Centre, Glenn Jordan, Chris Weedon, Marco Gil-Cervantes and - last but not least - my childhood friend and ex-student, Molly Maher, provided indispensable advice and help.

Despite all these combined efforts, some matters remain obscure. We do not know the identity of R. Jamadeesis, nor even the place of his death in Spain. To judge by his name, he may have been one of Tom Davies' Somali seamen; or, perhaps, he was 'the Arab boy' in his mid-teens who went to Spain - as still vaguely recalled by one or two people in Butetown. Of others who figure in the Table (see p. 121), we have no information about Dan Murphy or J. Taylor, both killed near Gandesa during the Ebro battle in July, 1938. Len John spoke at meetings after returning from Spain. J.K. Widdess makes a ghostly appearance in Hywel Francis' book. The 'boy from Cardiff, I never knew his name, a small, thin little chap'[2], remembered from the prison camp by Tom Adlam, may have been one of these last two, since both were among a group captured in March, 1938. Lastly, six other men apparently survived the war: their names are all we have - H. Body, Harold Davies, M. Levin, Tom McNulty, R. Stickler, W. Ward. I dedicate the book to these unknown soldiers and fellow-Cardiffians, not in order to glorify their cause (or causes), but to emphasise the sad fact of their anonymity. Let the bell toll for them.

Glossary and Explications

One of the legacies of the 1930s was a complicated political vocabulary - 'like letter soup' as a Spanish commentator put it. I have tried not to confuse readers with multiple initials of trades unions, political parties and other bodies, but occasional use of them is unavoidable.

B.U.F. - British Union of Fascists (Mosleyites, Blackshirts)
C.E.D.A. - *Confederación Espanola de Derechas Autonomas* (Conservative Alliance Party)
C.N.T. - *Confederación Nacional de Trabajo* (anarchist workers union)
C.P.G.B. - Communist Party of Great Britain
N.U.S. - National Union of Seamen
P.C.E. - *Partido Comunista de España* (Communist Party)
P.N.V. - *Partido Nacionalista Vasco* (Basque Nationalist Party)
P.O.U.M. - *Partido Obrero de Unificación Marxista* 'heretical' communist party, strong only in Catalonia
P.S.O.E. - *Partido Socialista de Obereros Españoles* (Socialist Party)
S.W.M.F. - South Wales Miners Federation ('the FED')
T.G.W.U. - Transport and General Workers Union
T.U.C. - Trades Union Congress
U.G.T. - *Unión General de Trabajo* (Socialist Party trade union)
Cortes - The Parliament of the Second Republic
Euskadi - The Basque word for the Basque nation
Euskera - The Basque word for the Basque language

The International Brigades:

Organised worldwide by the Comintern (the Third International, controlled by Stalin), there were a total of five brigades. The British Battalion (16th, later 57th) belonged to the 15th Brigade, and was sub-divided into companies. Other British volunteers served with brigade-level units, such as the anti-tank company. (Non-Stalinist socialists fought with other units, like the P.O.U.M. militia). The Brigades fought in every major campaign of the war, except that of the 'Basque' front. They were among the most reliable units of the Republican army - especially important during the defence of Madrid in winter, 1936-37. By the autumn of 1937, however, native Spaniards began to outnumber foreigners in all battalions, as the casualty-rate climbed higher and the tempo of recruitment sank lower.

The Foreign Legion (or Tercio):

Unlike the famous French outfit - on which they were originally modelled - they were not made up mostly of foreigners, but rather of Spaniards dedicated to the army as a career, as distinct from mere conscripts. Nonetheless, thousands of non-Spanish volunteers joined up in 1936, coming from backgrounds, and acting for motives, just as varied as those of the Internationals. They enjoyed privileged status in terms of pay and conditions, but lived according to an internal discipline which can only be described as ferocious. Their fanatical courage stemmed from a purely military more than a strictly ideological ethic. Until the latter stages of the war, their presence and that of their Moorish auxiliaries (*regulares*) was a pre-requisite for any important nationalist offensive.

Table of Events

Month/Year	Britain	Spain	Wales/Cardiff
January 1936	Death of George V Edward VIII succeeds		
February 1936	Public Order Bill bans 'political' uniforms	Popular Front government elected	
March 1936	Appeasement of Germany over Rhineland		
April 1936			Mosley rally in Pontypridd
June 1936	Seamen's Strike	*Armuru* incident	Anti-fascist violence in Tonypandy
July 1936	1.6 million still unemployed	Military Uprising	Over 12,000 men out of work in Cardiff
August 1936		Social revolution in loyal zone	
September 1936	Non-Intervention Committee set up	Basque Republic founded	Service for Spain in pro-Cathedral
October 1936	Hunger March to London		
November 1936		Franco attacks Madrid	King Edward visits South Wales
December 1936	Edward VIII abdicates George VI succeeds		First volunteers leave Cardiff for International Brigades Cardiff Aid Spain Committee formed

Month/Year	Britain	Spain	Wales/Cardiff
January 1937		Fighting around Madrid	Pat Murphy wounded
February 1937	Volunteering Outlawed	Battle of Jarama	Bill Coles killed
March 1937	Lloyd George supports Basques	Battle of Guadalajara	
April 1937	Chamberlain succeeds Baldwin	Basque campaign begins	Largest draft of Welshmen for Spain Capt Roberts and Fifi in Bilbao
		Guernica bombed	
May 1937	Public Opinion swings against Franco	Republic claims all merchant shipping	May Day Pro-Republic demonstration in Cardiff Frank Thomas wounded
June 1937		Bilbao falls	Refugee crisis begins
July 1937		Republican offensive at Brunete	Pat Murphy wounded again - Sid Hamm killed Spanish ships dispute in Cardiff Royal Visit to Cardiff Basque children in Carleon and Cardiff
August 1937		Santander falls	Luis Cicero escapes *Seven Seas Spray* impounded at Sañtoa

Month/Year	Britain	Spain	Wales/Cardiff
September 1937	Government resists pressure to end Non-intervention		
October 1937		Gijón falls - end of northern campaign	Joe Larreta captured Luis Cicero rejoins republican army
December 1937		Battle of Teruel	
January 1938			Joe Larreta in Teruel
March 1938	Appeasement of Germany over Austrian Anschluss	Aragon campaign	Calaceite disaster - Gilbert Taylor killed
April 1938			Several Cardiff POWs in Burgos camp
May 1938			Joe Larreta sent to Burgos camp
July 1938		Last Republican offensive - battle of the Ebro	J Taylor, D Murphy killed
August 1938	Czech crisis		
September 1938	Munich Agreement with Germany		
October 1938		International Brigades demobbed.	
November 1938	British rearmament stepped up	Defence of Catalonia collapses	

Month/Year	Britain	Spain	Wales/Cardiff
January 1939		Fall of Barcelona	
March 1939		Intra-Republican fight leads to fall of Madrid War ends on 1st April	

Chapter One: Cardiff's Immigrants and Spain

The Docklands

In the late nineteenth century the businessmen of Cardiff were fond of boasting that the maritime-industrial economy over which they presided was second only to that of New York City. Cardiff itself officially achieved the status of a city in 1905. Profit and wealth, along with the headlong physical growth and notable advancement of culture they brought to the metropolis, were the substance of civic pride. We should not underestimate the contribution of this great Victorian value to the shaping of Cardiff. Once again today, its citizens must draw heavily on the spirit of civilised competition if we want to flourish as a community - but this time, with a difference.

To the leaders of society a century ago, the words 'culture' and 'community' had much more restricted, exclusive meanings than those understood by most of us today. Perceptions of the city's life and future did not embrace the many dimensions of human experience represented in the narrow, noisy streets of Cardiff's docklands - the very area, as it happened, where most of the city's wealth was actually generated. Of course, the comparative claim about New York, in terms of a material economy, simply could never be proved - neither then nor now. What is more demonstrable is that the Cardiff of 1900 had the richest ethnic and cultural mix of any city in the world. In the decade leading up to the First World War, Wales was the only country in the world, apart from the U.S.A., to register a net surplus of immigration over emigration. Moreover, Cardiff's demographic infrastructure was more widely-based than that of Lower Manhattan. As Gwyn Alf Williams put it, 'Cardiff's Bute Street became the jugular vein of capitalist Wales'.[3] A casual amble along the length of Bute Street was likely to yield the observer an exotic variety of sensations which would have made Broadway, though ten times longer - and having the further advantage of two sides! - seem monochrome by comparison.

But in 1905, the complex *cultural* consequences of *economic* explosion were only dimly appreciated, and even then in a negative sense. The presence of ethnic minorities was regarded by most worthy citizens as an evil necessity, a rather unpleasant by-product of enterprise, something like the mess of metallurgical dross dumped at night on the Splott foreshore of the Dowlais Works. The dominant popular representations of foreigners and strangers -

3.
Looking up Bute Street, towards the city centre, from the Pier Head 1937.

in this age of Boxer Rebellion and Boer War - were wholly inimical to understanding. Years later, in 1937, when civil war was raging in Spain, the conference of the National Association of Head Teachers was held in Cardiff. At great expense, a presentation volume was compiled and published on behalf of the City Council by the Oxford University Press, for presentation to conference delegates. Its 250 pages and ten specially-commissioned chapters dealt with every aspect of the city which was officially regarded as having significance at that time. The various immigrant groups were granted a single passing reference, which occurred in Professor Marquand's contribution on 'Industry and Commerce':

> [Cardiff's] dock labour was largely provided by Irish immigrants, whose descendants today still constitute the bulk of the population living near its docks. Seamen and firemen of all nationalities also came into the port ... so that it would be true to say that one in every hundred persons in Cardiff is coloured.[4]

Tale of Two Cities

It is evident, therefore, that until the 1960s, the area becoming known in the nineties as Cardiff Bay was a bubbling site of what were, in every sense of the term, sub-cultures. Amongst these largely ignored communities, the Spanish element was growing steadily in the years before the First World War. In those hard times, few people had the inclination to know or care very much about such origins; nonetheless, links between Wales and Spain extended so far back in time as to vanish into the age of legend. After some debate on the issue, Spanish historians now accept that the earliest organised (and organic) societies of Spain were ethnically Celtic. Traditional bardic sagas tell of these tribes resisting Roman invasion with the same determination as Caradog the Welshman - or, for those with a healthy scepticism about legends, Asterix the Gaul. The Celtiberians staged desperate, suicidal last stands against the Romans and put up a fierce (to use an appropriate, if anachronistic, term) guerrilla resistance to foreign colonisation. Today, the only area of Spain which retains substantial archaeological evidence, and a living cultural tradition, descended from the Celtic epoch is the province of Galicia, occupying the north-west corner (as it were) of the Iberian peninsula. This is the region where Francisco Franco y Bahamonde, future leader of the Nationalists in the Civil War, was born and nurtured in the 1890s. But peoples of the Basque lands (*Euskadi*) too - although their mysterious language (*Euskara*) apparently has no connections - retain a vague affinity with things Celtic, perhaps the most evocative being their quasi-druidic primitive religion, with its prominent veneration of trees. Thus the ancient oak, historic symbol of the Basque spirit of liberty, located in the town of Guernica (in Euskara, Gernika).

As early as the seventeenth century, merchant shipping out of the South Wales ports began to creep down the Biscay coast of France as far as San Sebastian, capital of the Basque province of Guipúzcoa. By the later part of this century, a period when the kings of both Spain and Great Britain were called Charles II, records reveal the occasional importation of iron ore mined in Vizcaya into Cardiff, via the Spanish province's main port and capital, Bilbao. By this time, Bilbao had already locked into an economic take-off which was to make it the busiest port in the peninsula by 1800 - that is to say, at a time when Cardiff's similar development had not even begun. With the new century, however, the iron barons of Merthyr Vale began to strengthen contacts with Bilbao which - like much of their other efforts - inevitably stimulated the growth of Cardiff. By the 1860s, the pattern of coal outwards and iron ore inwards was being established. One of Cardiff's two largest shipping companies - the Morel Brothers, originally from Jersey - were the pioneers. As the 'biographer' of Cardiff's industrial history informs us:

> They part-owned over 100 sailing ships trading to France and Spain,

> taking out iron and coal and returning with pitwood and potatoes. To these imports were added Spanish ore, which Morel Brothers were among the first to develop. They were chartering up to 120 vessels a month in addition to those they owned. In 1876 they acquired their first steamship, and others followed built specially for the Bilbao iron ore trade. They not only shipped ore but also invested in Spanish mines.[5]

The voices of Cardiff-based seamen were regularly heard along the banks of the Nervión, Bilbao's arterial river estuary; and the local architecture of the Basque city began to reflect British styles in fashionable suburbs like Portugalete - Bilbao's equivalent of Penarth - where the ship-owning and shop-owning families built their grand houses, away from the polluted atmosphere of the crowded, insanitary docklands. By a coincidence of destiny, Bilbao's population had grown in the same way and to the same extent as that of Cardiff. Bilbao grew by sucking in the poor and huddled masses not only of its immediately neighbouring regions, but also from distant Andalusia - in this context, the 'Ireland' of Iberia. If we include the chain of smaller dockland settlements built along the Nervión estuary towards the sea, the Basque capital had grown to over 100,000 souls by 1900. It now represented one of the two major industrial conurbations in Spain. Moreover, things so turned out that Bilbao's hinterland economy as a whole was highly complementary to that of Cardiff. Of course, the demographic maturation of the Welsh partner was more recent besides being even more dynamic. With a mushroom spurt of growth which still seems astonishing, Cardiff had more than doubled in size, from 80,000 to over 160,000 in the last twenty years of the nineteenth century alone. In the 1890s, the building of the great new iron- and steel-making factories on the Cardiff East Moors initiated a period of close contractual links with Bilbao for the supply of high-grade ore. In its turn, the Spanish port, by now a major shipbuilding and global trading centre, was anxious to preserve its supplies of Welsh steam-coal and anthracite.

The late Gwyn Alf Williams once pictured the situation with no more than his normal ration of excited hyperbole:

> Not only did John Cory's bunkers straddle the world and South Wales keep the Royal Navy afloat, the capital, technicians and technology of South Wales acquired world power. They helped to distort the development of Spain, wrenching its heavy industry base away from Asturias into the Basque lands where Cardiff and its hinterland were entrenched in Bilbao.[6]

4.
S.S. Portugalete in 1900

Cardiff, too, had built ships, though this industry failed to become established in the face of stiff competition from other British centres. Early in the age of steam, the *Mallorca* had been the first iron steamship built in the town's yards. By all repute one of the most splendid vessels ever to be launched in Wales, it was constructed in the Bute yard, which occupied the site of the future Curran works on the banks of the river Taff, and was launched in November, 1864. The vessel was commissioned by the Spanish Royal Mail Line, for use between Barcelona and the Balearic Islands. As late as 1900, the significantly-named S.S. *Portugalete* set forth on its maiden voyage, as the latest addition to the Morel merchant fleet which traded mainly with Bilbao. In addition to these contacts, by 1900 Cardiff had developed links with ports in the south of Spain, such as Huelva (Andalusia) and Cartagena (Murcia).

The Latin Quarter

Until the 1880s, the peninsular presence in Cardiff - I refer now to its human dimension - was sporadic and transient: the occasional crew on shore leave from a Spanish ship in dock, the occasional individual sailor on a longer visit, after having jumped ship, or having been left behind after ending up in the Cardiff calaboose. The onset of industrial depression during that decade - a world-wide phenomenon to which South Wales, thanks to its uniquely-valuable coalfields, proved relatively immune - brought the first genuine immigrants. It was no accident that perhaps a majority of the families of Spanish descent who were to be established in Cardiff by the 1930s came originally from the wider hinterland of Bilbao. They may have begun their odyssey by travelling to Bilbao after uprooting from one of the villages of the interior or - as bachelor seamen - from one of the dozens of fishing villages spotted along the Vizcayan coastline. Men who failed to find work in Bilbao itself sometimes decided to take ship for South Wales. After coming ashore, many first of all travelled onwards to centres of employment away from Cardiff, attracted by work in Merthyr ironmaking or among the coalmining villages of the Swansea valley. But several such families had resorted to Cardiff within a generation, some driven again by economic necessity, others by the need to have a life among a larger society of Spanish friends and familiar customs - a drive which sometimes had a religious aspect. The main point was that Cardiff now offered a much wider variety of opportunities for immigrants than any other town or region of Wales. Contraction in one employment area could always be compensated by expansion in another, whilst a large service sector was coming into being. As the Spanish-speaking community increased in size, it brought a range of economic and social advantages for its members. Families helped each other out financially, established formal business links and in time, intermarried. The healthy state of Cardiff-Spanish commerce encouraged the growth of trades which provided services for Spanish ships and seamen, and by the 1920s no fewer than four ships' chandlers firms belonging to Spanish families were established.

It was probably for this reason that most Spanish families settled in the narrow terraced streets leading off James Street to its south (or seaward) side and connecting the latter to Stuart Street. In particular, George Street and Louisa Street were favoured, since they provided almost the nearest domestic

5.
Cardiff Docks area in the 1930s, with the pattern of streets to the south of James St clearly visible.

6.
A group of Spanish immigrants on their way to South Wales in response to the Crawshay Company recruitment drive in 1907.

dwellings to the dock gates. Such proximity cut down delivery time for stores (and consequent expense) whilst, at the same time, encouraging visiting seafarers into eating-places and boarding-houses where a familiar cuisine and a friendly welcome were guaranteed. Extended family and employees of the business firms naturally lived as close as possible to their places of employment. By the time of the First World War - which was to have the effect of increasing the tempo of trade with Spain - between fifty and sixty Spanish families had their location and daily being in Butetown and the Docks, more than half of them in the two streets already mentioned. In the central year of our story - 1937 - the Cardiff Directory records that eighteen out of forty-four houses in George Street were occupied by persons with Spanish surnames. Little wonder that one writer refers to the area as 'Cardiff's Latin Quarter', while another recalled:

> We had a Japanese family, we had Portuguese, Irish, English, Greeks, North Walians and a lot of the Spanish Armada, who were mostly living in George Street, but we were all boys and girls, no different to each other and playing happily together. When Frankie Mayo's granny shouted to him 'Ven Aqui' we all knew that the answer in Spanish was 'Que Quieres?'.[7]

Among the best-known residents of the Latin Quarter were the Perez family, who had migrated from the tiny village of Huergas de Gordón, near Ponferrada in León province (northwestern Spain) in the early years of the century. José

María Pérez was a struggling small farmer, who had been pushed to desperation point by the deaths of two children from typhoid fever in infancy. The region around Ponferrada boasted established centres of iron-ore and coal-mining. And in 1907 the management of the Cyfarthfa works advertised in the town, looking to import cheap labour in a period of increased wage-demands among domestic workers. Perhaps encouraged by friends who already had some industrial experience, José María decided to take his family to Merthyr Tydfil. There, conditions of life may have been different - but in some respects they were little better; Florentina Perez lost another two babies, but at least managed safely to nurture Josefina and Peter. Later, in 1919, the family moved down to Cardiff and invested some savings in a small business. By the 1930s, the Perez shipping stores and bakery business in George Street was not only a thriving concern but also the most popular social centre for all the Spanish community. This establishment has been recalled with affection in more than one published memoir of the Docklands in these years, and is vividly profiled in a recent (and almost 'official') history of Tiger Bay:

7.
'Fina' Perez behind the counter in George Street in 1956.

> Josephina Perez was without doubt a prince of general stores. 'Josey's'- the memory of that little general store, even today, brings a far away look into old people's eyes. The smell of fresh baking bread, chorizos, beans, peanuts and *cocido* stew cooking on the family stove, combined in a dance of delight that tickled the taste buds ... She sold salt fish that was fit for a king, thick and white with grains of salt glittering like small diamonds. Now, years later, people swear it has never been surpassed. Josey cooked her salt fish and called it *bacalao* - a dream of a dish with olive oil, garlic, onions and herbs.[8]

In the 1930s, Louisa Street-born Bill Twamley was friendly with Josefina's brother, Peter, who took care of the delivery side of the business. At the time, Peter was courting Bill's sister, Doris:

> His father had a model 'T' Ford which Peter used to drive ... 'Jose Perez and Sons' it said, Bakers and Wine Merchants and we kids used to ask him for a ride and he couldn't very well say no ... We'd go over the dock to take provisions to the ships there: bread, lovely warm smelling Spanish bread; bottles of wine and oil; and sacks of vegetables and sometimes all the way over to Barry Docks.[9]

In a newspaper feature of 1956, Josefina explained her own feeling for Cardiff: 'three times I have been to my own country. Each time I have longed to return to Cardiff, where all my friends are'. By this time, she was married to one of her more appreciative customers, a Basque sailor named Hormachea. Only forty families were left, of a community which in 1920 had reached towards twice that number. Nevertheless, 'Josie' ('Fina' to her Spanish friends and family) maintained her business well into the sixties.

> In George St you would have found Perez' Wine Shop, Josefina ('Josie') Hormachea's famous salt fish (aromas still recalled by local inhabitants) and a Spanish restaurant... Josefina served meals to Spanish seamen who fancied a meal in her big family kitchen ... at any given time twelve to fourteen people would be sat around the huge oak table in the room behind her saltfish shop.[10]

Another Spanish ships' chandler located in George Street was that of Santiago Isidoro. This firm was apparently more successful (at least in this department) than the Perez outfit, since - as Bill Twamley recalls - 'They had a bigger lorry ... Another of the gang, "Beato", drove that for his father and this lorry was used in the summer to take all the mates camping down in Lavernock'[11]. Not far away, in Patrick Street, Mr. Munitiz operated yet another similar enterprise, whilst nearby in Bute Street itself, the Del Guerra family ran a workshop which made and sold all types of oilskin wear for seagoing mariners and local fishermen. This enterprise also enjoyed a contract to supply the city council to equip its out-of-door workers with rainwear. Given the terrible recession in Cardiff-based maritime commerce in the 1920s, the fact that so many enterprising families continued to drive a business, mainly from services to Spanish ships and sailors, is in itself a testament to the robustness of the links between Cardiff and Spain (and, by extension, the Spanish-speaking world of South America). Indeed, right down to the late 1950s, over a dozen vessels were still regularly engaged in the transport of iron ore from the Galician ports of Corunna (La Coruna) and Vigo to the furnances of Port Talbot and East Moors.

Some other immigrant families had thrived mightily in the fat years before the Great War, to the extent that they could afford to move out of the Docklands area into more salubrious suburbs, like Grangetown. Such were the Avilez family (probably hailing from the port of Avilés in Asturias) who lived not far from the recently-completed new Catholic parish church of St. Patrick. Nearby, for a time, lived the even more successful Bicarreguis, a Basque family, originally chandlers, who had profitably diversified by themselves acquiring shipping interests in Cardiff and Newport. This family at some point moved residence to the latter town, though retaining a strong business presence in the Docks.

For many less fortunate immigrants, life was harder and more precarious. The parents of Maria (Mary) del Mazo came to Cardiff with her mother's brother in 1910. They took ship in Bilbao, where her father already had experience as a steelworker, in the middle of a desperate economic depression. The couple had originally left the town of Soria in Old Castile, where Antonio Machado (who later, at the time of the Civil War, was regarded as Spain's greatest poet) was earning his living as a schoolteacher. At exactly this juncture, Machado was writing his evocative lines about Spain's decline from imperial greatness:

> Castile......
> ...wretched in its rags, despising what it does not understand.[12]

Once established in 'Imperial South Wales', Maria's father and uncle got jobs in the Dowlais steelmills, and she was born during the Great War. During the postwar depression which - in its turn - brought devastating and sudden economic collapse to Cardiff, the father and uncle absconded to Argentina, and were never heard from again. Later, Maria's mother married Jose Sanchez, who had been resident in South Wales since the 1860s, and was probably one of the earliest Spanish immigrants. He had worked in the old Dowlais works in Merthyr until it closed. He then came to Cardiff, but failing to be taken on at East Moors, instead signed on as a sailor. After his ship was lost with all hands in 1929, Mrs. Sanchez took in lodgers in their house in Louisa Street. It was there that Luis Cicero, Maria's future husband, came looking for a contact in 1940, knocking on the door just as the sirens were sounding for one of Cardiff's first air raids.

José (Joe) Larreta was also born in Cardiff during the First World War. His parents came to Cardiff (via Bilbao) from two small villages in rural Vizcaya - his father from Ichurriega, his mother from a farm near Mungia (in the *comarca de Butrón*). They arrived in or around 1904, with one daughter. They kept a boarding house in Loudoun Square, where they grew very close to another Basque family living next door, the Barracaldos. In 1921, when Joe was just five years old, the whole family returned to Spain because his mother, who had contracted an incurable disease, wished to die in her native land.

But, as things turned out, and unknown to him at the time, young Joe had not escaped his prescribed destiny as a Cardiffian and denizen of Tiger Bay.

The Cardiff Irish

Another section of the Cardiff population, with, on the face of things, little or nothing to do with Spain, was to become involved in the world-wide emotions and the local divisions generated by the Spanish Civil War. These were the citizens of Irish origin, some of whom could already trace their family's residence in the city back for four generations by the 1930s. They were densely settled in the wider Docklands area - including areas like Newtown, Grangetown and Splott which contained between them perhaps 60 per cent of the city's 20,000 Irish-affiliated citizens. The reasons for the interest in Spain's Civil War manifested within this community were religious and economic. People descended from Irish immigrants were usually Catholic; and their religious loyalty was - at least in terms of practice - more fervent and more public than that of their Spanish co-believers. On the other hand, the great majority of this community still belonged to the economically-deprived sections of the city's population, and in the mid-1930s this could often mean near-penury and daily hardship. There were exceptions, of course: like the Purnell family whose undertaking business thrived to the extent that they produced Cardiff's third Catholic - and Tory - Lord Mayor in 1937. Nevertheless, other things being equal, the Cardiff Irish were firmly behind the Labour Party and strong in their support of the trades unions. They were a radical breed, if ever there was one. But the onset of the Spanish Civil War - a conflict Alonso Sanchez has called 'a religious tragedy' - meant that other things were no longer equal.

Apart from individual friendships, formed in the classroom of Catholic schools as children or between adults working in Catholic charitable organisations, there was little contact between the Spanish and Irish communities. In particular, their respective social behaviour was still very different. Although the landlords of one or two pubs in the Latin Quarter were Spaniards (the Gomez family kept 'The Pilot' in George Street for a time) on the whole the Spanish immigrant male was slow to acquire the habit of pub-going and tended not to join labour or other organisations which might be regarded as 'political'. In contrast, among the Cardiff Irish such 'joining' and public self-identification was much more usual, and men took a voluble interest in such issues as Irish

Home Rule, as well as the politics of their adopted country. However, apart perhaps from those Cardiff-Irish sailors engaged in the Spanish trade, there was little background knowledge of or interest in Spain as such.

A partial exception to this rule existed in the Welsh Catholic diocesan custom of sending young men who had a vocation for the priesthood to seminaries in Spain - above all, to St. Alban's in Valladolid (north-central Spain). This venerable institution had been founded in the sixteenth century as a Jesuit college for the training of seminarians from the British Isles, but had passed into the hands of the secular clergy in the eighteenth century. In the 1920s it was run by an Irish administrative staff, so that the second- and third-generation Irish Cardiffians who made the pilgrimage felt (in a way) at home when they arrived at this exotic city in the middle of the vast Castilian plain. In 1938, whilst the Spanish Civil War was still raging, two young seminarians returned to visit their old school (St. Illtyd's College) in Splott: the school magazine reported that 'they are keeping the Illtydian colours flying in Valladolid where they are preparing for the Sacred Ministry'[13]. Some years earlier, Fr. James Hannon (future Bishop of Menevia, the Catholic diocese of North Wales) had studied for the priesthood in Valladolid. Unlike the majority of his colleagues, he took the opportunity to learn Spanish, in the city which is the equivalent of Dublin in the English-speaking world - for it is said that *Vallesoletanos* practice the most perfect spoken Castilian known to man. Valladolid was (and still is) also one of Spain's more conservative cities. In 1934, it was to be the scene of the final formation of the Spanish Fascist party (*Falange Espanola*), via the fusion of various extreme right-wing groups. It was long before this juncture, however, that James Hannon had returned to Cardiff to be ordained; and in the mid-thirties he occupied an influential post on the staff of St. David's pro-Cathedral in Charles Street. At an earlier stage of his career, however, he had been a curate in the Docks, officiating at St. Cuthbert's Church, and had built up warm relations with Spanish and South-American families. Norrie Russ (née Barry), who attended St. Cuthbert's School in the twenties, remembers that every other child in her class seemed to be Spanish. Fr. Hannon would hear their confessions - along with the perhaps more interesting ones of itinerant Spanish seamen - in their own language. He is recalled as having a good knowledge of political developments in Spain and perhaps followed the turbulent course of the Spanish Second Republic in the early 1930s. For most of his flock, whether Spanish or Irish, their being caught up in the terrible dispute of 1936 came suddenly and unexpectedly - but the event was to prove important in his life as in theirs.

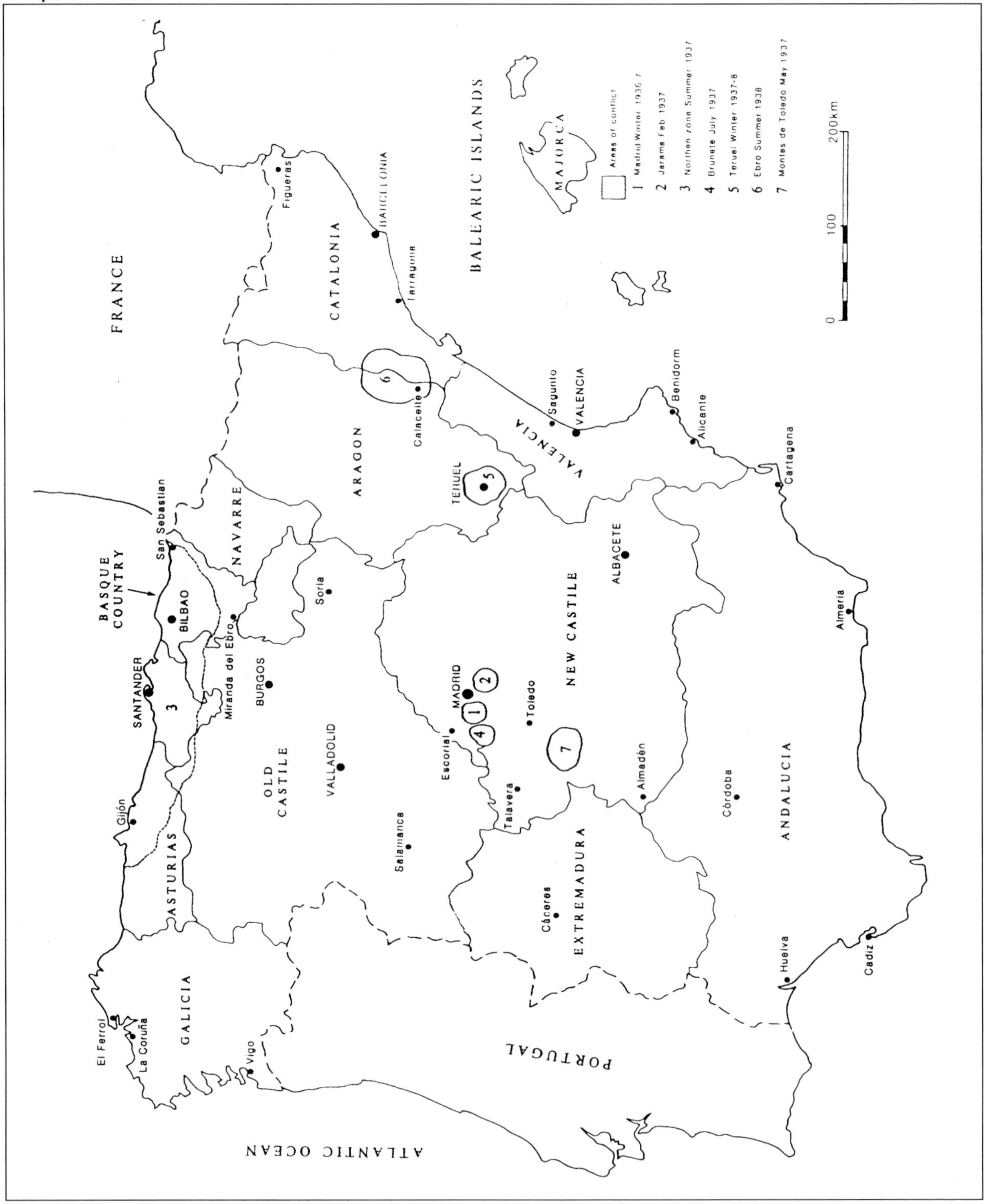

Map I.
Spain and the Balearic Islands, with places mentioned in text.

Background to Civil War

In the years when the founders of the Cardiff Spanish community took the momentous decision to uproot themselves from their *patria* (mostly, that is, between 1900 and 1914) an enormous number of immigrants - over 100,000 - arrived in South Wales. They came from every continent in the world. As with the overwhelming majority of immigrants since the dawn of time, it was sheer economic necessity - the survival instinct - which drove men and women from Spain to leave their homes, friends and familiar surroundings. It is doubtful that many of them were political refugees seeking asylum, in anything except the most indirect sense.

Spain in the early years of this century was an odd political specimen: a kind of semi-demi-democracy, a constitutional monarchy, but one with a severely restricted franchise and a closed electoral system. In most regions of northern Spain a species of power-broker called the *cacique* (the local landlord) ruled over political arrangements, usually with the collaboration of the Civil Guard (armed police) and sometimes, too, that of the parish priest. Though conditions of life and labour for the unprivileged masses in these provinces were not as dreadful as in the arid, poverty-stricken south, the rural economy as a whole had been in serious recession since the 1880s. There was a continuous movement of population within the peninsula. Thousands of under-employed landworkers left Andalusia to find employment in the industrial belt around Barcelona - which was still expanding rapidly - but also in the now less economically buoyant Bilbao area, thus further decreasing prospects for the local population. These and other tensions led to constant industrial disturbance, a situation exacerbated by the defeat of Spain's armed forces by the U.S.A. in the war over Cuba and the Philippines in 1898. Humiliated abroad, the army tried to restore its reputation by taking a stronger role at home; at the same time, the labour organisations, both socialist and anarchist, began to flex their muscles, and pro-revolutionary activity increased. It may have been the permanent threat of confrontation and violence in Catalonia - which burst to the surface with frightening consequences in 1909 and again in 1917-20 - which persuaded many to leave Spain altogether rather than take their chances in the bear-pit of Barcelona.

The Spanish socialist party (P.S.O.E.) had been founded in 1879 and not long afterwards it was complemented by the formation of a national horizontally-organised trade union, the U.G.T. At the same time however, anarcho-syndicalism (the C.N.T.) grew rapidly in the south and east, dividing the labour movement bitterly, and, as it proved, irreparably, against itself. In contrast to Barcelona, the industrial ports of the northern provinces - Bilbao, Santander (Cantabria) and Gijón (Asturias) - tended to be socialist-dominated. Two Spanish-Cardiffians, Luis Cicero (born 1908), a Castilian from the Santander region, and Jose Larreta a Basque who grew up not far from Gernika, were P.S.O.E. supporters as young men, and they both admired the dynamic leader of the party in Bilbao, Indalecio Prieto (himself an immigrant to the city from Asturias). During the First World War, neutrality brought substantial economic benefits to Spain and this upturn was maintained - though at a much lower rate - through much of the 1920s. In 1923, however, after prolonged violence in Barcelona seemed to be leading to social revolution or to a Catalan declaration of independence (or both), the army overthrew the pseudo-democratic system, and King Alfonso XIII accepted the dictatorship of General Miguel Primo de Rivera. The P.S.O.E., having refused the call from Moscow to join the Third International, parted with its communist wing, and established its non-revolutionary, 'reformist' credentials. Under the direction of Francisco Largo Caballero (leader of the U.G.T.) and Indalecio Prieto, the Party adopted the tactic of working peacefully, within the terms laid down by Primo de Rivera's regime, in order to achieve important elements of its social programme. In this course it was remarkably successful.

8.
The Socialist leader and minister, Indalecio Prieto.

Primo's relatively benign dictatorship came to an end with his resignation in 1930, and in the following spring local elections in many regions demonstrated a widespread rejection of the monarchy. A revolutionary situation quickly sprang up in Madrid, and with the advice of his army chiefs the king decided to leave the country, becoming Spain's most celebrated - if hardly most typical - emigrant. The Second Republic was now established (an abortive First Republic having existed in 1868-72). Its democratic government was dominated by a coalition of middle-class liberals and socialists, and immediately embarked on a programme of social reform. The Republic's intentions were sincerely high-minded and its legislation considerably improved the economic circumstances of the poorer classes. But the fundamental issues of reform - i.e., the role of the army in society, more equitable landownership, and the privileges of the Church - were handled with insensitivity and/or incompetence. The Republic managed to alienate the economic and religious establishment, whilst at the same time exciting the expectations of its working-class supporters beyond any possibility of rapid fulfilment. Even its own thoroughly proper democratic aspirations rebounded on its head. For example, the introduction of female suffrage made possible the defeat of the reformist coalition in the general elections of 1933, since most Spanish women - regardless of social background - were deeply conservative, and cast their votes accordingly. The new centre-right government had a tenuous hold on power, and in October 1934 was obliged to admit members of the ultra-rightwing Catholic party (C.E.D.A.) into the cabinet. This move precipitated a series of violent protests by socialists and separatists. In the coalmining valleys of Asturias this turned into nothing less than bloody social revolution, a situation which dramatically foreshadowed the forthcoming events of 1936.

After the savage repression of the Asturias insurrection - masterminded by the ambitious young General Franco - the Madrid government abandoned any pretence of reformism. In 1935, in desperation the leftwing opposition regrouped into a 'Popular Front', a broad alliance of middle class and workers' parties which was joined by republicans, separatists, socialists, communists, and eventually even the powerful anarchist movement, which until then had bitterly opposed all governments of whatever political complexion. It was this broad and ramshackle alliance which defeated the right-wing government in the general elections of February 1936 - but only by the narrowest of margins. From the start, the authority of the new government was undermined by the refusal of their more radical hustings partners to join the Republican parties in the cabinet. Spain became dangerously polarised, whilst its middle-class cabinet was increasingly isolated. On one side, the defeated right refused to accept the veracity of the election results, whilst on the other the triumphant left could not contain the revolutionary ardour of their supporters. Despite the bloodletting in city streets between police, fascists and socialists, and direct action against unpopular landowners in the countryside, the government struggled to stave off social chaos, whilst at the same time renewing the reform programme left unfinished in 1933.

Tremors of the Earthquake

One interest-group which the new government tried to satisfy was the Basque National Party (P.N.V.) which had thrown its weight behind the Popular Front. A statute of devolution, granting autonomy to a government of the Basque country, was introduced into the Madrid Cortes (Parliament) and debated in the summer of 1936. Eventually passed, despite the desperate opposition of the right-wing, it was due to be implemented after the summer parliamentary recess. Another sector of society overdue for reform was that of maritime commerce. Spanish seamen, a labour-force which was mostly recruited from strong pro-government regions (the Basque country, Catalonia, Andalusia), had for generations suffered appalling conditions of service. In May, 1936, the government issued a decree (pending a full legislative process) which imposed on shipowners the obligation to introduce radically improved conditions for sailors. The owners - in the circumstances of the worst trade depression in history - were not prepared to comply. Though Spain's increasingly desperate political situation had evoked little public comment in Cardiff, this news was different. The *Western Mail* reported it, from a management-biased standpoint which reads oddly today:

> The new conditions of employment ... were extremely onerous, and many Spanish owners were reported to have decided to lay their boats up ... The manning side was to be greatly increased, while the men were to receive a substantial increase in wages and work was limited to eight hours per day. Further, the new terms provided for improved accommodation for crews, a month's holidays with pay each year [and other benefits]. The Spanish steamer *Santi* recently chartered [in Cardiff] to carry coal to Malta, has been laid up.[14]

The resulting dispute was a mixed blessing for Cardiff. Shipowners were anxious to exploit the opportunities offered by the dispute if to do so was feasible and lawful: Cardiff, after all, still had fifty-seven different shipping concerns, owning 143 vessels between them. The docks labour force was naturally keen to benefit, as long as it was felt that to do so was morally acceptable: in 1936, after all, unemployment in Cardiff stood at nearly 12,000, and was actually to rise further before the end of the decade. In trading terms, too, the dispute was a mixed blessing. On the one hand, it meant - at least potentially - an increase in local business, but on the other, many Spanish firms soon found it even more difficult than usual to discharge their debts to South Wales suppliers.

In response to what perhaps should be termed a bosses' lock-out, the Spanish Seaman's Union declared a strike. The worst affected port in Britain was Workington, where the British United Steel Company provided blackleg crews for five Spanish ships, and local 'communist agitators' and police confronted each other on the decks - that is, on what was legally 'foreign soil'. In Cardiff docks, a strike of crew members on board the S.S. *Armuru* (and at least one companion vessel) also caused considerable disruption. The crews sent envoys to the local Trades and Labour Council, which resolved to support the strike 'in every way possible' - in effect, giving it the same status as an official 'domestic' dispute, and thus taking a stand against employment of 'scabs'. The national situation became serious enough for the Home Office to show concern, and a meeting between the interested parties from various ports was held at Whitehall in early June. Cory Brothers, the Cardiff-based shipping company, sent a representative to complain that the strike restrained them from discharging a contract for the *Armuru* to deliver 4,000 tonnes of coal to Marseilles. At the same time, Welsh shippers sent a joint deputation to the Board of Trade to ask the government to put pressure on Madrid: some firms were already owed nine months' arrears of payment from their Spanish customers.

The timing of these events was significant, since the summer of 1936 was one of exceptional political activity and sporadic industrial protest in South Wales. A large-scale hunger march on London was being organised by a 'popular front' of left and labour organisations. Oswald Mosley's party (the B.U.F.) was beginning to make some headway in the port towns, and even - whisper it softly! - in Merthyr Tydfil. In Cardiff, crowds drifted on summer Sunday evenings towards the southern entry to Llandaff Fields, the area conveniently near a busy tram terminus. Here an imitation Hyde Park Corner event would ensue, often punctuated by untidy scuffles in the place where the Fascists raised their banner and their voices. Cissie Conway recalls walking to Llandaff Fields with a group of young people, after evening service of Benediction in St. Patrick's Church, in order to watch young Catholic men strutting their stuff in black shirts. Violent clashes were taking place everywhere in South Wales where the Mosleyites tried to organise meetings. The words 'fascist' and 'communist' were constantly on people's lips, and they became part of the everyday vocabulary even of those who had no special political commitment. However, there could hardly have been many people in this latter category in 1936. The propertied classes lived in fear of 'red' revolution; the unemployed masses nurtured much resentment at wealth and privilege. As if this were not enough, the leaders of *Plaid Cymru*, including one Dr. Saunders Lewis, an ascetic lecturer in Welsh at University College, Swansea, were hatching a plot to deal a sensational blow against the English military establishment. Events in Spain were to twist all these tensions into a knot. The affair of the *Armuru* with its menacing sub-text of a possible blackleg crew to be hired by the Cory Company, did little to dampen a smouldering mass of grievance and frustration in South Wales, which threatened at any moment to burst into flames. Looking back, the vessel seems like a messenger from hell, herald of the tragedy to come.

Franco's Cardiff Dragon

For as it happened, the conflagration of class war and violent nationalist uprising was actually ignited, not in Cardiff, Swansea and Merthyr, but in Madrid, Barcelona and Bilbao. Yet although five hundred miles from the scene of the action, Cardiff was in the midst of things right from the start. In early July, 1936, a group of Spanish monarchist exiles in London were looking for a pilot to fly to the Canary Islands, ostensibly on a business publicity jaunt. In fact, these men were part of a deeply-laid conspiracy, seeking to piece together the elements of an uprising against the Republic, to be spearheaded by the professional army which was mostly based in Spanish Morocco. Unfortunately for the plotters, the best man to lead this force was its co-creator, Francisco Franco, who had been (in effect) exiled by the Republican government, sent out of harm's way to command the garrison of the remote Canary Islands. After being approached by the rebels, the Olley Airways Company of Croydon contacted one of their staff. The man they chose was Captain Cecil Bebb, who hailed from Church Village, and had been educated at the County School in nearby Pontypridd. To this day, his family are still involved in the transport business in the Cardiff area - though in a perhaps less glamorous line than aviation was in the 1930s. In 1936, Bebb was an experienced ex-R.A.F. pilot in his early thirties, working as a freelance in the south-east. He had been selected by destiny to be the chauffeur of the Francoist regime in Spain.

An amazing journey ensued. The mastermind behind the plan to pick up Franco from his distant Atlantic exile and reunite him with his army in Morocco, was Luis Bolín, a brilliant journalist who later became Franco's press and propaganda expert. The plan was audacious and risky: several fuel stops had to be made, which in turn meant encounters with international police and airport authorities; moreover, a few days of bad weather could have ruined the whole operation. It was hardly a surprise that in 1986, fifty

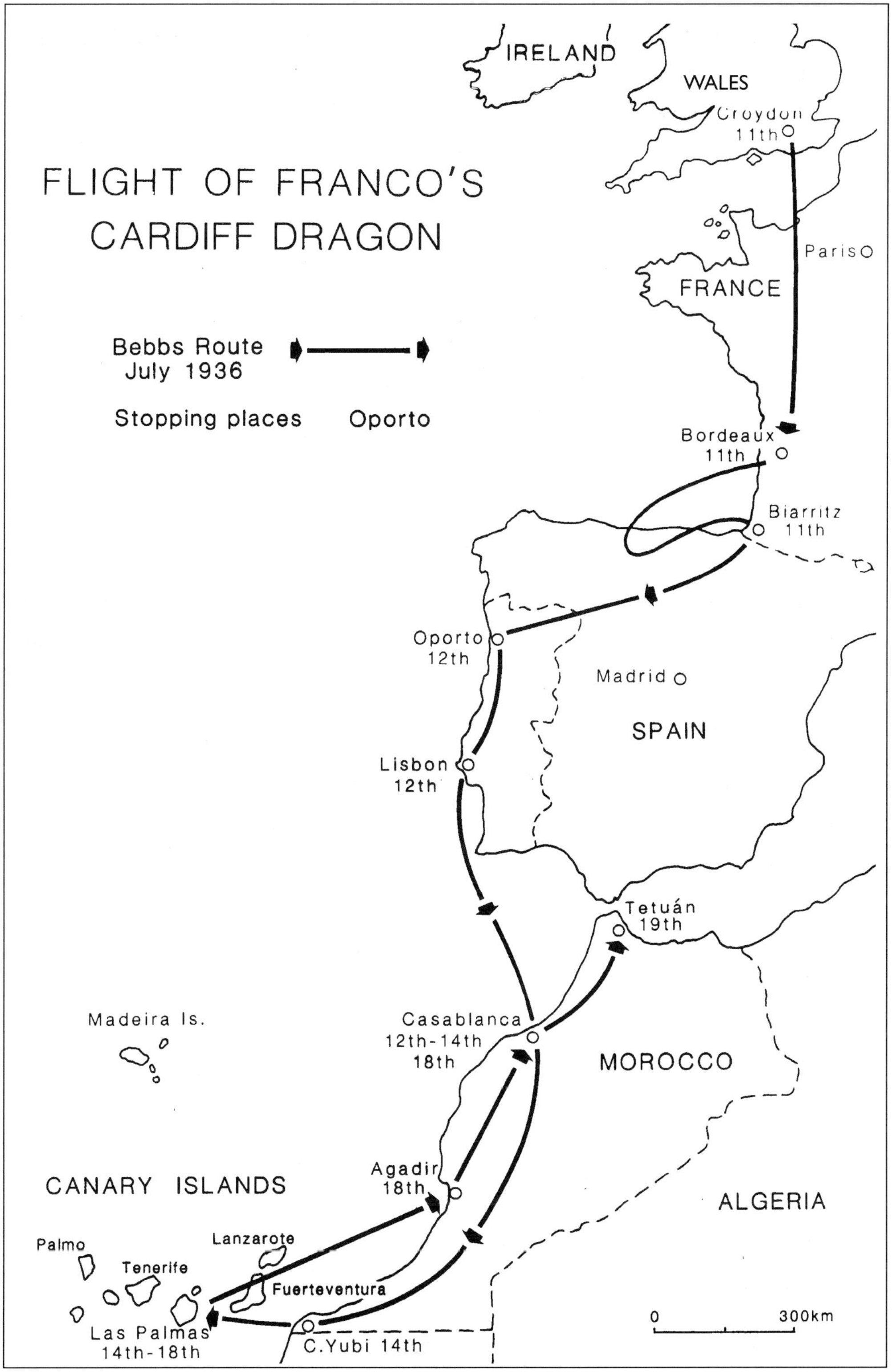

Map2.
Flight of Franco's Cardiff Dragon.

years later, a feature film loosely based on the incident was released in Spain, with great success. As part of the cover, two attractive blonde 'extras' were included in Bebb's party - seen as necessary matching accessories of aeronautics in those days (as with expensive fast cars today). Bebb's machine, a De Havilland Dragon Rapide, was a costly item, in effect a luxury small airliner carrying seven passengers. The whole trip was bankrolled by the Catalan millionaire Juan March, a dedicated enemy of the Republic.

The plane left Croydon airport early in the morning of 11th July. By now, Bebb had been told that his mission was to collect an Arab leader from exile, so that he could lead an insurrection in Spanish Morocco: it was like being part of a 'Boy's Own Paper' story of war in the desert, 'a lovely challenge'[15] as Bebb later recalled his reaction. After they had arrived at Las Palmas, one of the girls wrote to a friend 'I am having a mild flirtation with the pilot, who is a redhead'[15]. Shortly afterwards Bebb woke up from this idyll and realised that things were not as innocent as had been pretended. The man who was hurried across the runway into his plane was evidently no Sheikh of Araby, nor for that matter a Beau Geste. On 17th July, with the payload of General Franco on board, Bebb took off again and headed for Morocco. On that same day, events in Madrid had prematurely sparked off the military rebellion. Following the assassination of the rightist politician, Calvo Sotelo, the secret signal was given. Morocco was already in the hands of the mutinous army, and rebel troops had taken over in the streets of several towns in mainland Spain itself. At the very time that Bebb touched down at Tetuán - dawn on 19th July - the Madrid government recognised that its only protection from the army was the people, and accordingly began issuing arms to thousands of trade unionists in Madrid and other cities. The terrible response to military rebellion was social revolution: for months to come, Spain would be turned into a bloodbath of terror and counter-terror. 'One day you will know what you have done'[16], said Bolín as he embraced Captain Bebb on the runway at Tetuán, at the successful end of their mission. A red-head from the unofficial headquarters of the Welsh 'Reds' - Pontypridd - had been the innocent carrier of civil war, flying in his strangely well-named Dragon Rapide.

9.
Franco united with his army

Chapter Two: The War Comes to Cardiff

Events and Opinions

When the military uprising began in July 1936, most regions of northern Spain quickly declared an allegiance to the Republic. Though some rebellious garrisons held out (especially in Asturias, where officers believed they could expect no mercy from the vengeful miners) the apparently secure possession of these industrially and strategically vital regions was at first regarded as a decisive blow against the insurgent generals. In Santander and Gijón, the dockworkers and other proletarian groups, led by the U.G.T., seized the initiative - though it is true to say that a majority of *Santanderinos* were at heart more in sympathy with the rebellion than the Republic. In Bilbao, pro-Republican dominance was guaranteed by a working alliance of the Socialist and Basque Nationalist parties. Though the bishops tried to remain neutral, large numbers of the secular clergy were immersed in Basque cultural nationalism, and in many villages of the strongly Catholic Basque countryside the parish priest usually sided openly with the people. A few months later, with the full permission of Madrid, the P.N.V. leader, José Aguirre, was to declare the existence of the Basque Republic within a federal, democratic Spain, and to become the first President of 'Euskadi'.

Opinion in South Wales, as reflected in the local press, was for some time confused and uncertain about the situation in Spain. This is not surprising, since the situation itself was anything but simple, and both the quantity and quality of news coming out of the country was unsatisfactory. In Cardiff, the *South Wales Echo* and the *Western Mail*, as well as carrying the usual Reuter-syndicated stories about military events, also succumbed to the general weakness for atrocity stories, and particularly those which concerned the murder of priests. During the second half of 1936, in many parts of Spain - though against the wishes of the central government - a ghastly massacre of clergy took place, as part of an almost indiscriminate purge of suspected reactionary and 'fascist' elements. Many foreign newspapers carried travellers' tales which were luridly exaggerated and merely calculated to excite outrage. This in turn - other things being equal - was likely to evoke an anti-government sympathy in the reader. With hardly more background knowledge of Spain than the ordinary person on the Pier Head tram, the editorial and news staff in St. Mary Street were hard pressed. They had frequently to pinch themselves, for example, in order to remember that the ill-organised and motley masses on the newsreels, many of them - quite literally - preaching anarchy, were the forces of the legal government, whilst the parade-ground soldiers marching resolutely to brush them aside were actually the rebels.

In the *South Wales Echo*, the foreign correspondent, Harry Greenwall, carried a flag for the Republic and

> considered himself something of an expert on the subject. He also wrote in a way which gave the reader the impression he was a personal friend of all the leaders of Europe and regularly obtained their secret plans.[17]

Despite extensive coverage, Greenwall's reports on the military situation, reflecting blind confidence in a government victory, were wholly ignorant of Spanish politics and geography, and as a result often farcically inaccurate. In general the editorial policy of both Cardiff-based dailies was to maintain a stolid official neutrality. Yet at the same time, they grasped the opportunity to emphasise the terrible consequences of social breakdown and class hatred; thus they (quite properly) underlined a moral message for the readership on both sides of the social divide.

Yet almost from the first there was a discernable sympathy for the Basques, even in Cardiff's more comfortable drawing-rooms and clubs. It is important here to draw a distinction between the main (Popular Front) government in Madrid (later established in Valencia, and later still in Barcelona) and the geographically-separate northern region - dominated by the Basques - which also opposed the rebellion. In South Wales, even Franco supporters had a grudging regard for the Basques. Part of the reason was the commercial links which had been forged over the previous half-century, and even - to put it crudely - the business instinct itself. Some felt that an autonomous Basque state would be good for business. Others saw immediate opportunities in the supply of Spanish ports with all kinds of necessities imposed by war; and others still, more passively, hoped to preserve their investments in the Basque economy. Many were impressed by the fact that the fledgling Basque Republic was under the control of an effective and moderate government - Bilbao being the headquarters of the moderate wing (named 'Prietista', after Indalecio) of the P.S.O.E., who made common cause with the conservative P.N.V. Observers noticed that political terror and anti-clerical atrocity were not major features of Republican resistance in this part of Spain. Of course, there was also support for Basque national aspirations in Wales - at least a vague empathy with a small (some alleged 'Celtic') nation, a country of coasts, hills and valleys, struggling for freedom against overwhelming odds.

But this too seemed strange when the main spokesman of Wales's own Nationalist Party (*Plaid Cymru*) professed himself an admirer of Franco. Saunders Lewis, in common with many - but unusually for an intellectual and writer - came to regard General Franco as the saviour of Christian civilisation in Spain. This was perhaps understandable in view of his personal conversion to Catholicism: though his version was virtually a different religion to that of the South Wales Irish. At this very time, Lewis was planning his celebrated attack on the bombing school in the Llyn peninsula, which was to lead to his being sacked by University College Swansea, and a (later) relocation to the Welsh Department at Cardiff. Meanwhile, in June 1936, the *Western Mail* announced the appointment of a new assistant lecturer in the History Department at the University College in Cathays Park. Dr. Christopher Hill was to become one of the most active and influential historians of postwar Britain. A convinced Marxist with an Oxford background, he was already at work on an appropriate book - about Lenin and the Russian Revolution. Taking up his teaching post in October, Dr. Hill immediately became involved in the committee of the 'Aid Spain' movement (see below). At a more senior level, too, the academic response was at variance with that of Saunders Lewis; the College Principal, Frederick Rees, and Professor Marquand of Economics, also publicly expressed their support for the Republic.

Organisation and Action

The main initiative and central dynamic of commitment came not from the intellectual elite but from working-class organisations. Indeed it was the local branch of the Communist Party which, having failed to persuade the Trades Council to take action, proceeded to call a general meeting in Cardiff on December 18th. From this gathering emerged both a South Wales Council for Spanish Aid and a Cardiff 'Provisional Spanish Aid Committee'. As Hywel Francis' account states:

> The work of collecting foodstuffs, clothing and money began immediately. The same night over eleven hundredweight of food and

> clothing was sent from Cardiff to the Spanish Food ship which was about to sail from Southampton.[18]

For those days of poverty and social deprivation, this was an impressive gesture. Before very long, with the cautious involvement of the Labour Party and the Trades Council, branches of the committee had been set up in every electoral ward in Cardiff. Door-to-door collections could now be organised in virtually every street. A taxi-driver from Swansea who had transferred his business after marrying a Cardiff girl, joined the Communist Party around this time. Harry Stratton put his vehicle at the disposal of party and aid operation, and devoted most of his leisure time to collection and delivery from the main base in Collett's bookshop in Castle Arcade.

All this pro-Republican activity was - if not actually unlawful - frowned upon by officialdom. The British National Government, headed by Stanley Baldwin, had set a course which led in the autumn of 1936 to an International Agreement on Non-Intervention in Spain. In early August, the Prime Minister, having turned down an invitation to attend the annual music festival at Gregynog Hall (Montgomeryshire) a few weeks earlier, accepted a supplementary offer made by its owners, the Davies sisters, to spend a few days there on his own, recuperating from the cares of office. However, hearing of Baldwin's presence in Wales, Harry Pollitt, secretary of the C.P.G.B, determined to upset his holiday. He ordered party officials in South Wales to organise a petition, calling upon the P.M. to reconvene Parliament in order to discuss the crisis in Spain. Will Paynter headed the delegation which took this document to mid-Wales in early August in Harry Stratton's taxi. (Both these two, and another member of the delegation, were later to join the International Brigades.) As Stratton recalled,

> When we arrived [at Gregynog] the delegation succeeded in handing in the petition, in spite of the attentions of a truncheon-wielding policeman in the grounds of the Estate! Afterwards, the delegation held a public meeting in the centre of Newtown in support of the Spanish Republic, and later we heard that the presentation of the petition, asking Baldwin to recall Parliament, had been recorded on the B.B.C. news.[19]

Nevertheless, the interruption of the 'rude mechanicals' had not flustered the First Lord of the Treasury, who 'much appreciated the peace and quiet of

**10.
Lord Plymouth receiving the freedom of the city of Cardiff, October 1936.**

Gregynog, finding deep delight in the grounds and gardens ... the butler looked after his every wish'. Before leaving for London and his main political preoccupation - the consequences of Mrs. Wallis Simpson - Baldwin planted a copper beech tree to mark his visit; it died within a few weeks.[20]

The non-intervention policy meant that both the legally-elected republican government and its enemies were banned from receiving any aid of strategic significance. In modern war, of course, almost any aid has strategic significance, but under the Non-Intervention Agreement only medical provisions and food supplies were exempted from the ban. The Cardiff Provisional Aid Spain Committee thus came up against the Non-Intervention Committee, comprising representatives from many nations, and to which Baldwin - not without interests in Cardiff - appointed the earl of Plymouth as chairman. Lord Plymouth was a prominent local worthy, virtual owner of Penarth (not to mention much of Grangetown) and master of St. Fagan's Castle. Perhaps he had found himself with time on his hands at this point, since Penarth Docks, which his father had been instrumental in constructing, had been forced to close for lack of business that very year. At any rate, Cardiff City Council took the opportunity to show its approval of both Baldwin and his nominee by granting the latter the freedom of the city not long after his appointment as the world figurehead of non-intervention.

One man who objected to everything that the noble lord stood for was Jim Henson, local representative of the International Transport Federation - an umbrella organisation of transport workers' unions. Henson was keen to obtain collaboration so as to deny port facilities and dock services in Cardiff to all shipping bound for destinations in Nationalist Spain with the aim of trading with the rebels. His efforts met with only limited success. In reply to feelers from his London headquarters on this issue he wrote, 'I regret to state that I think it would be useless for you to ask any assistance officially in the fight from the N.U.S. or T.G.W.U'[21]. He also expressed doubt that Cardiff transport workers and dockers as a whole, though in principle sympathetic to the Republic, would be likely to 'black' such ships unless their own local union executives sanctioned it. All the same, in the winter of 1936-7, Henson was able to work with the Norwegian seaman's union branch in Cardiff, and with the Spanish consul, Señor Clemente Cebada, to prevent the departure of several vessels for Francoist Spain, whilst also lobbying effectively against recruitment of blackleg crews.

In political terms, the pro-republican campaign in Cardiff had come to resemble the situation inside the Spanish Republican government itself. Having moved from besieged Madrid to Valencia, the latter became more and more dependent on Soviet military aid, along with the dynamic and ruthless commitment of the Spanish Communist Party (P.C.E.) to ultimate victory in the war against the nationalist rebels. The grip of the Comintern (the Third International, controlled by Stalin) on affairs in the government zone thus tightened steadily, and soon the P.C.E., under its direction, was cohering and controlling the whole republican war-effort. This leadership, however, involved the gradual suppression of the views and influence of other constituent parties of the Popular Front. Henson reflected a similar tension, in microcosm:

> It seems a great pity over here to see the attitude of some unions and the Labour Party on this question, especially as, on the other hand, the Communist Party are working in all ways to help Spain. On the Cardiff Spanish Medical Aid Society we are all working together at assisting and have no time to fall out politically, whilst it seems that our leaders, with a few exceptions ... seem to be waiting ... until Franco, Hitler and Mussolini arrive in London.'[22]

This last sentiment suggests that Henson, Will Paynter, Christopher Hill and their comrades accepted the argument that unless Franco was stopped, his allies, the European fascist dictators, would be able to march inexorably towards the conquest of Europe. Or, as Edgell Rickword, editor of the celebrated *Left Review* - in an uncannily accurate and menacing vision - expressed it:

> In Hitler's frantic mental haze
> Already Hull and Cardiff blaze,
> And Paul's grey dome rocks to the blast
> Of air torpedoes screaming past.[23]

As can be seen from Henson's letter, the sanctions of non-intervention had already obliged the committee to change its name to something more in accord with what was now - in effect - international law. But Henson's experience also suggests that opposition to its work was strongly entrenched within the official labour movement. After initial doubts, the local Trades Council had been persuaded to endorse the Aid Spain Committee, but later its secretary told Walter Citrine, secretary-general of the T.U.C., that they had been misled into believing that the T.U.C. was involved, and they withdrew support again on receiving a pamphlet from the committee attacking both the T.U.C. and the Labour Party.

But - as might be expected - opposition to the steps taken by Jim Henson and his allies was not limited to sources within the labour movement. The authorities were also anxious to discourage action which may have aggravated public feeling, and adversely affected the conduct of business. But, by the very nature of the exercise, discretion (or, if your prefer, secrecy) was the order of the day. On one occasion, Steffen Greve, Cardiff official of the Norwegian Seamen's Union, was visited in his office by two men dressed in civilian clothes.

> The men sought to point out to him the unacceptability of the seamen joining the boycott and pressed him to persuade - or order - them to rescind their decision and honour their obligations to their employers. Greve pointed out that such decisions were made on board ship by the crew themselves and not by the union as such. Moreover, it was outside the power of the unions to order its members to carry out actions - policy was made by the members. Apparently, the plain clothes visitors then began to indicate the vulnerability of Greve's position as a foreigner involved in a politically motivated dispute. At this point, Greve asked the men to wait for a moment while he got his hat and coat, and invited the men to accompany him to repeat their statements

> in front of a magistrate. The visitors protested that his reaction was quite excessive and uncalled for and, as the conversation quickly petered out, they left the office.[24]

Greve clearly, and with good reason, suspected his visitors to be Special Branch detectives.

Whilst these difficult waters were being negotiated, it was the Communist Party alone - in Cardiff, as in a thousand other places, obeying the orders of Moscow - which went ahead with recruitment of volunteers to fight for the Republic in Spain itself. Such action was deeply controversial within the labour movement, and (although at first the legal situation was cloudy) was soon to become actually criminal. Though the majority of the volunteers themselves hailed from the politically-embattled coalfields, Cardiff was the centre of the operation. In back rooms of the leftwing bookshops, both Collet's and the official C.P.G.B. shop in Charles Street, interviews of volunteers were held, registration documents were filled in, secret travelling instructions and papers issued, cash-in-hand for the trip doled out. Not long before Christmas 1936, the first groups were sent off to London on the first stage of their journey to Spain. Most of this work was carried out by Len Jeffries and Will Paynter (Paynter himself later served as political commissar in Spain). During the first half of 1937, small parties of up to half-a-dozen men were able to leave Cardiff General station on a regular weekly basis, and recruitment was especially heavy during the period of the Basque crisis that spring. On one occasion in April a platoon of twenty-seven men were waiting - with little chance of appearing inconspicuous - on the platform for the Paddington train. Though detectives of the Cardiff City Police did at times call on suspects' families, and doubtless the Special Branch knew what was happening, active police intrusion was generally avoided. The Communist Party may have ironically appreciated this version of non-intervention, but it was certainly no sign of official favour. As far as the police were concerned, it was simply much better for potential class warriors to make their war in Spain than in Cardiff.

Equal and Opposite: The Catholic Reaction

It was not just the Conservative-dominated National Government, the municipal ruling class and even the mainstream labour movement, who were opposed to such overt demonstrations of support for the Republic. In a leader at the end of July, a mere fortnight after the uprising in Spain, the *Welsh Catholic Times* had warned its working-class faithful against giving money for schemes to aid Spanish workers, since it might be spent 'on petrol to burn churches':

> For ourselves [this editorial added] we do not regard the rebels as necessarily proved defenders of the Catholic Church ... but it is quite clear that the Government of Spain and its main supporters are venomous haters of the Church.[25]

The Archbishop of Cardiff, the Rev. John Mostyn, issued a carefully-worded pastoral letter on 13th August, asking God 'to grant that this hatred of religion may cease in Spain'[26]. Shortly afterwards a special service was held in St. David's Cathedral, attended by 'many members of Cardiff's Spanish colony'[27]. Fr. James Hannon preached in Spanish to the congregation:

> Today, Spain is an immense blazing conflagration. Our immediate task is to smother the outbreak. Later, when the danger is past, the day of reckoning for the guilty will come ... I don't ask you to take up arms, but to join your hands together...[28]

Only a few weeks later, Fr. Hannon, despite his qualifications in Spanish and experience in the Cardiff Docklands, was transferred to become parish priest at Aberavon. In his public choice of phrase, and in the minds of some members of the congregation, he had evidently moved too close to the Francoist side, and too far from the necessary spirit of forgiveness. Even in his new posting, Fr. Hannon seems to have transgressed his own earlier statement about taking up arms. In November, a young man wrote to General Franco offering his services on paper headed 'Port Talbot Hotel, Aberavon':

> My reasons for writing are; first of all I am a Catholic, in fact a daily communicant, a statement my parish priest will endorse. Second ... for seven years I was at a famous Welsh public school, Christ College, Brecon, before proceeding to Sandhurst ... My age is 21 and I am willing to accept any position ... to act as a spy, or perhaps you need an English wireless announcer.[29]

The parish priest of St. Illtyd's church in Dowlais was rather more circumspect than Fr. Hannon. Addressing the Catholic Young Men's Society, he called on Catholic members of the Labour Party and working class organisations, not only to disavow but to resist 'publicly and emphatically' any attempt to provide aid for 'Red Spain'. 'Only thus', he maintained, 'can they acquit themselves of the guilt of sharing in another's sin'[30]. Dowlais, which still retained sizeable Irish and Spanish Catholic groups, was a major centre of pro-'Red' activity; but the answer to Fr. Dalton, whose sermon was reported in the *Welsh Catholic Times* came from an Irish docker in Cardiff:

> As a member of the Labour Party and a Trade Unionist let me assure him that we are fully alive to the danger, and we have not all been silent ... There are a few thousand Catholic men fighting for a living on Cardiff Docks ... It is absolutely necessary for us to be members of a Trade Union to protect ourselves, and at all times ever since I have worked on the Docks, we have had to fight the anti-Catholic element ... In regard to the money that has been sent to Spain ... Catholics like myself in the three Trade Unions - that is the coal trimmers, railwaymen and transport workers - have protested and although we have been beaten, because we are in a minority, our presence is felt.[31]

An overwhelming majority of the Catholic faithful in Cardiff were of Irish descent; and nearly a century after the arrival of their pioneer forefathers to construct the Bute Docks, they still formed (by and large) the poorer element of the working class. A majority of the breadwinners were, as Mr. Daly's letter suggested, unskilled or semi-skilled docksmen, at the mercy of the fluctuating demands of the job market; others worked in heavy industry, and still others were seamen. Unemployment among the thousands of Irish-Catholic families in Newtown, Grangetown, Roath, Splott and Canton was higher than the average. Roy Denning, who grew up in Canton, recalled:

> They had strange names that all began with 'O' or 'Mac', they belonged to large families, they tended to be poorly dressed, and were dangerous if provoked. Their homes were a rent-collector's nightmare.[32]

Given that all these families were indeed 'fighting for a living', there was a strong temptation for men to respond to an invitation to infringe the then-dominant codes of industrial relations by servicing 'blacked' ships or joining 'scab' crews. This inclination was all the keener since many, even where unwavering in their support for the Labour Party, had little sympathy with the ideological reasons behind pro-Republican action of the kind advocated by Jim Henson. Many Catholic breadwinners were in a cruel predicament. It was one thing to refuse to connive at aiding the Republic; but quite another for families to suffer loss of earnings, and consequent privation, as a result of acting in solidarity with a policy which they instinctively found repugnant. As Tom Buchanan, historian of the labour movement's reactions to the Spanish War, has demonstrated, a vocal minority of working-class Catholics all over the country began to manifest a sense of identification with General Franco. Only his leadership, they believed, could bring to an end the persecution of their religion in Spain. The struggle against 'the anti-Catholic element' - entrenched religious prejudice - and the identification with a folk-culture through which they often endorsed the cause of Irish Catholic-Nationalism, gave working-class Cardiff Irish a sense of empathy with victims of persecution in Spain. It was a spirit exceeded only among the nationalist community in Northern Ireland.

This stood in contrast to other parts of Wales, where the enthusiastic collaboration of nonconformist leaders with left-wing politicians was a notable feature of the Aid Spain movement. Such zeal could sometimes be more the result of latent distaste for Catholicism than positive sympathy for the cause of Spanish workers. Similar distaste was sometimes manifested in Spain by Welsh members of the International Brigades, men who themselves had often disavowed the nonconformist beliefs on which they were suckled. In certain circumstances, Cardiff-Irishmen were also quite capable of turning their backs upon the faith of their fathers - or, at least, of setting aside the advice of the clergy - in favour of more powerful feelings of working-class solidarity. It is notable, for example, that four of the twenty or so Cardiff International Brigaders had Irish surnames. On the other hand, the present writer can testify to the admiration for Franco often expressed inside Catholic circles during the post-1945 epoch, when the negative consequences of the Soviet triumph for religious practice in Eastern Europe were often contrasted with the much more satisfactory situation in Spain.

Such tensions were of course religious-cultural in origin rather than political. Nevertheless, religious leaders were aware of the potential for divisions both between and within confessional-ethnic groups. Some parish priests were more concerned to defuse this situation than others. In the event, in terms of political action - even at the ballot-box - the implications of the Spanish Civil War were limited. Whilst it seems established among historians that throughout the U.K. Catholics were more likely to join fascist movements than others - in Leeds, for example, Mosley's nickname was 'The Pope' - only a minority of

Cardiff Catholics came to see Mosley as a crusading saviour of Rome. Some who did join the B.U.F., such as John O'Neill of Grangetown, achieved prominence.

No-one among the Cardiff Spaniards went this far, although some families were known to have pro-Franco sympathies in 1936. This caused divisions, sometimes publicly expressed, among the community. In choosing sides, the coincidence of religious feelings (or the lack of them) with economic status appears to have been decisive. This operated in favour of the Franco side in the cases of the Isidoro, Bicarregui, Avilez and Perez families. Others, whose businesses depended on maintaining contact with Bilbao, were Nationalist supporters more by default than conviction, especially after the fall of the Basque Country to Franco in 1937, when not to evince such support would be to risk harming livelihoods. On the other hand, poorer families and especially those with an unemployed breadwinner, were often pro-republican. Perhaps the best-known focus of this cause was the cafe kept by Pepita Campos, voluble in support of the Republic, in West Bute Street. Over coffee in the bar the partisan discussions were sometimes heated - especially as Pepita's husband, a Basque ex-skipper named Jaregui, was not of her persuasion. It was to Pepita's cafe that Ben Evans came on several occasions in 1937-8, in order to leave and pick up clandestine messages exchanged between Basque refugee children domiciled in Cardiff and their parents in Bilbao. The exercise was carried out in classic cloak-and-dagger style, the packets being left in the gents' toilet, in order to avoid attention from potentially unsympathetic eyes. Evans was a steward, and sometimes cook, on the Constant Brothers ships (the so-called 'Inge' line) which had resumed trade with Bilbao after the fall of the port to the Nationalists. Once in port, Evans would carry his precious burden (along with supplies of *bacalao* - Spanish-style salt fish) to a parish priest who was his secret contact in the Basque capital.

Since the Spanish community had never developed its self-consciousness to the extent of forming public societies or associations, political feelings, however strongly they may have run, mostly remained muted and underground. On one or two occasions - it is true - they surfaced in a big way. Several Cardiff Spaniards were recruited onto the Aid Spain Committees and doubtless it was these committed Republicans who marched shoulder-to-shoulder with their comrades through the city centre on May Day, 1937. Perhaps in reaction

11.
Cardiff's pro-Republican Spaniards marching in the May-Day parade of 1937.

to this, political slogans supporting the Franco side were daubed in huge letters on the Bute Street railway embankment, near the present Letton Road underpass. The perpetrator was apprehended - maybe through information provided by the other side - and received a stiff jail sentence. Later on, during the post-Dunkirk panic of 1940 and Churchill's policy of 'collaring the lot', some pro-nationalist families were required to evacuate their homes and take up residence at least twenty miles from the city. Several families, for example - including those of Perez, Isidoro, and Lepategui - were settled for a year or more in the Abergavenny area. After Fr. Hannon's departure, it appears that the Catholic clergy were careful not to exacerbate feelings among both Spanish and Irish faithful. However, in July 1937, Archbishop Mostyn officially opened a new Catholic Seamen's centre. It had been fitted out at a cost of £750 with money raised by the lay charitable society of St. Vincent de Paul, doubtless including contributions from both Irish and Spanish parishioners. The new premises were appropriately placed on a corner of Bute Street between Bicarregui's stores and Patrick Street. 'It is essential', said the Archbishop, 'that a Catholic atmosphere be provided for seafarers - a large number of whom are Catholic'[33]. Exactly two weeks earlier, Franco's troops had occupied Bilbao, and by the autumn the same fate had befallen both Santander and Gijón. The Catholic Seamen's Institute was soon to be not short of customers forcibly exiled from their home lands and ports.

Orphans of War: The Basque Refugees

In the spring of 1937, the nationalist invasion of Vizcaya - largest of the Basque provinces - led to a surge of sympathy for their plight in many parts of Great Britain. The doyen of Welsh politicians, ex-prime minister David

Lloyd George, made a celebrated speech in the House of Commons expressing his solidarity with the Basque people, using a vocabulary imitated many years later by President Kennedy in West Berlin. The saturation-bombing of Guernica, the first attack of such a nature on an undefended town, changed attitudes to Spain (and to war itself) almost overnight, and evoked world-wide condemnation. Feeling was overwhelmingly directed in favour of the Basques as such, rather than in blanket support of the Spanish Republican cause in general. Nevertheless, the effect was to increase the standing of the latter, and commensurately to diminish the pro-Franco interest. Then, in the last week of June, child refugees from the Basque country, consigned by their parents to the care of various aid organisations, and numbering over 4,000 in all, arrived in Southampton.

Plans were immediately laid to bring some of these 'orphans of the war' to South Wales. The Cardiff Aid Spain Committee negotiated with Monmouthshire County Council for the loan of 'Cambria House' in Carleon, which was converted for use as a hostel-cum-boarding school. The organisational (and to some extent, financial) driving force behind the operation was the pro-Republican, Liberal shipowner, J.E. Emlyn-Jones. Some carers and teachers - like Christopher Hill - provided their services free of charge, but the post of director was necessarily a full-time appointment. It was taken by Cyril Cule, a specialist in Spanish language and literature, who had actually been in Madrid, waiting to take up a teaching appointment, when the Civil War broke out. Despite on one occasion nearly being shot by a militia patrol, he was a keen supporter of the Republic and had only left the capital on the British embassy's urgent advice. His job at Caerleon paid a princely ten shillings a week - perhaps twenty pounds today - (and full board!). But the fifty-odd children brought to Cambria House were a costly commitment. A new fund was opened in order to pay for reception, clothing and feeding, and other maintenance charges. With the support of the local press, this fund quickly flourished. One marvellous source of income was the soccer team formed at Caerleon. The Basque boys proved to have tremendous skills and their all-conquering run reached a climax in May, 1939, with a match against Moorland Road, the Cardiff Schools champions - including three Welsh internationals and one Ron Stitfall, full-back - at Ninian Park. This was a link renewed nearly fifty years later when another notable Cardiff soccer product, John Toshack, went to San Sebastian and a career of greater celebrity than any other foreign manager in Spanish football history.

NINIAN PARK, CARDIFF.
(By kind permission of Cardiff City A.F.C. Directors).

Nº 1348

WEDNESDAY, MAY 10, 1939.

Kick-off—6.30 p.m. by the LORD MAYOR OF CARDIFF,
(Alderman W. G. HOWELL, J.P.)

Captains A. COLLEY and JUAN ANTONIO HERNANDEZ.

MOORLAND ROAD SCHOOL
(League Champions and Senger Cup Winners).
V.
BASQUE BOYS
(from CAMBRIA HOUSE, CAERLEON)

E. Davies & Son, Printers, Paradise Place, Queen Street, Cardiff.

12.
Cardiff v Bilbao 1939: the two schoolboy soccer skippers.

The MATCH BALL, autographed by both captains, will be presented to the holder of the programme with the winning number.

RIGHT— **MOORLAND ROAD SCHOOL** *—LEFT*

W. TANDY†

G. SCAMMELL† R. REGAN

A. COLLEY† (*Capt.*) T. JONES†† E. CHORLEY

G. WILLIAMS G. WILCOX K. GRIFFITHS†† R. HOPKINS R. STITFALL

Referee: Mr. HAROLD WILLIAMS, Chairman of Cardiff Football League Committee.

†† These boys play for Cardiff and Wales.
† These boys play for Cardiff.

MANOLO ASENCOR JUAN BILBAO JOSE LUIS ACHA GABRIEL PARRON EMILIO ESPIGA

FEDERICO ESPIGA JUAN ANTONIO HERNANDEZ (*Capt.*) CARLOS ACHA

ANTONIO ASENSIO ARMANDO FERNANDEZ

ENRIQUE GARATEA

LEFT— **BASQUE BOYS** *—RIGHT*

Reserves—RUFINO GARATEA JULIO ANDRES

I want to thank all those who have made possible the humane work carried on at Cambria House. All through South Wales and Monmouthshire generous help has been forthcoming. Until the Basque children return to their native land, it is the desire of my Committee that they should be looked after with the same care and consideration as during the last two years. I, therefore, appeal for your continued support.

J. E. EMLYN-JONES, *Chairman*,
Executive Committee,
Basque Children's Home,
Cambria House, Caerleon.

4, Dock Chambers,
Cardiff.
6th May, 1939.

13.
Cardiff v Bilbao 1939: the line-up.

Early in their stay, the Caerleon children were entertained to tea by the Principal and Mrs. Rees on the lawn of University College in Museum Avenue. The party was joined by the Duchess of Atholl (popularly known as 'the Red Duchess' because of her support for the Spanish Republic) whose speech in the Cory Hall officially launched the fund. Also prominent in the campaign were Lord Davies of Llandinam, the millionaire coalowner whose father had commissioned Barry Docks. He and his sisters - owners of Gregynog Hall, which had earlier stood so forbiddingly in favour of non-intervention - had initiated the Welsh national fund with contributions of £1,500. By the end of July, Cardiff's fund had reached £500 (the equivalent of £20,000 today), by dint of donations from such sources as Cardiff and District Sunday School Union, Rumney Baptist Sunday School, the Bishop of Llandaff, and Grangetown Infants School. The cross-party nature of the sympathy evoked by the Basques is illustrated by the ten shillings received from Christopher Hill's colleague and friend in the Cardiff History Department, Dorothy Marshall - whom Dr. Hill today recalls (affectionately) as 'a terrible old Tory'!

Despite this pro-Basque 'popular front', the whole affair evoked intense controversy. Right-wing elements fostered the suspicion (perhaps not wholly without foundation) that the forced immigration of children was a propaganda ploy, calculated to cause outrage against the Nationalists. A heated correspondence ensued in the *South Wales Echo.* One writer condemned the 'pomp and show'[34] of hospitality to the Basques, when the native unemployed lived in poverty on the dole. In the week before the royal visit to Cardiff (July 1937), such choice of phrase was infelicitous, and invited the riposte that *this* 'pomp and show' should be cancelled and the money made over to the Basque children. However, contributions from the Catholic community to the Basque children's funds were notable by their absence. The *Welsh Catholic Times* referred to the children as 'tiny pawns in a propaganda game'[35], and rejected criticism by the *Western Mail* of its 'contradictory' policy on the issue. An outbreak of violent discontent at another South Wales home for Basque children (at Brechfa in Carmarthenshire), was reported by the Catholic newspaper under the headline: 'These "Basque Babies" are Red Terrors'[35]. A reaction followed in which rapid repatriation was recommended by several correspondents, and previously favourable leader-writers discernably wavered.

The effort put into 'Cambria House' was not the only indication of Cardiff's help for the Basques. Several dozen children were fostered into private homes in Cardiff and other South Wales ports. Joyce Howells (niece of International Brigader, Bill Coles) recalls that two little girls of around her own age, Conchita and Raquel, came to live with them in Tremorfa. Alun Emlyn-Jones (whose sister had been named Iñes in recognition of the family's business link with Spain) remembers a teenage boy who, similarly, came to stay at their home in Senghenydd Road. Though they naturally attracted the most obvious concern, the welcome mat was not put out solely for the 'orphans of the war'. A group of Basque fishermen who had abandoned their home ports with a flotilla of trawlers, ended up in South Wales, with the help of local sympathisers and the Spanish Aid front. Sometime in late 1937 or early 1938, Franco's diplomatic representative in London, the duke of Alba, despatched a secret agent to Cardiff to investigate the situation. Alba was evidently fearful that Cardiff, with its unique mixture of left-wing activists and pro-Basque sympathisers was becoming a dangerous focus for anti-Franco activity. The spy, Eduardo María Danis, probably operated under a commercial cover, and made contact with pro-nationalist expatriates in the city. It was around this time that Doris Perez, who had a room to spare, was asked by her sister-in-law, Josefina, to provide bed and breakfast for two mysterious Spanish gentlemen, 'Don Feliciano' and 'Eduardo'. The Perez home in Taff Embankment was placed conveniently near the Docks, and could be used as an ideal 'safe house', situated in a one-sided street, looking across the river towards what was then still open space which existed before the Curran works were constructed. Doris saw little of the two men, who were out on business all day. When they left, Eduardo told her he was going to London. But, of course, these events may be nothing more than a coincidence....

In April 1938, an official reported to Franco's foreign minister, General Jordana:

> The Spanish representative in London has passed on to me a communication from our sub-agent in Cardiff, accompanied by reports concerning the activities of certain Basque nationalist elements, along with others about the personalities of various Spanish persons who, on the contrary, have shown themselves favourable to our cause.[36]

Danis also reported that Basque trawlers were operating out of Milford Haven under the British flag - what a contrast to the attitudes of our own day! By September, 1938, with the aid of the pro-Franco lobby, Danis had cracked the telegram codes used by the republican consul, Clemente Cebada, so that

14.
J.E. Emlyn Jones with his son, Alun, and a teenage refugee from Bilbao being looked after in their Cardiff home, 1937.

15.
Basque refugee children on the lawn of Cardiff University College with their hosts, Principal and Mrs Rees.

the latter's messages could be intercepted in London. It may also have been Danis' presence in Cardiff which led to many Spanish seaman who were holed up in the docks for various reasons (see Chapter Three), resisting the attempts of the authorities to encourage their departure.

> Cyril Cule, who had taught at the Basque Children's home in Caerleon, was able to help some of the sailors. One man who, in Cardiff, was put on a ship for Spain against his will, jumped overboard and swam to Penarth, where he was maintained by the South Wales Miners, together with three other Spaniards, in a disused hotel, with Cule acting as interpreter between them and the S.W.M.F.[37]

These sailors hoped to ingratiate themselves locally by putting their experience of war to good use. Anyone with a claim to be Basque was now (after Guernica) regarded as an expert in aerial warfare - so the men offered to build air-raid shelters in Cardiff on an alleged Bilbao patent. However, the immigration officer, Mr. Reeve Jones (whom we shall meet again) was a stickler for the rules. He arrested some Spaniards and put them under restraint on a ship bound for Spain. The skipper, however, put the men ashore at Barry, where they got a more sympathetic reception.

But by the summer of 1938, enthusiasm among Cardiffians for the Basque cause had faded. Within five years, some ninety per cent of the original complement of child exiles had been restored to their homes, only around 400 remaining in Britain. Although the Civil War was not yet over, the inevitability of nationalist victory, and the dictates of human nature, combined to reduce public interest. In August, the *Western Mail* published an article by the marchioness of Bute reporting on a tour she had made through the nationalist zone of Spain - courtesy of Luis Bolín and the Franco propaganda office. She referred to the 'absolute normality of the country' which manifested 'everywhere the same spirit - that of a crusade'[38]. Before concluding that the *Western Mail* was reverting (as it were) to type, it must be remembered that, in the 1930s, the Bute family retained a major financial interest in the newspaper. Moreover, although Lady Bute was herself a Catholic from an Irish landed family - not quite the same culture as her co-religionists in Cardiff - one may doubt she actually believed the spirit of crusade to represent eternal normality everywhere in Spain. At any rate, her piece attracted a spate of hostile correspondence. Even the Heath Co-operative Women's Guild committee unanimously voted to find Lady Bute's opinions distasteful. She came under heavy fire from an ex-International Brigader, Thomas Evans of Kenfig Hill - and was duly defended by Frank Thomas, ex-nationalist volunteer from Cyncoed. Among other things, Evans' letter denied that the Republican Airforce had ever bombed open towns, but he was a victim of his own side's propaganda. In fact, indiscriminate civilian air attack had been initiated by the loyalists as early as August, 1936, with a raid upon the city of Granada. And - as Thomas pointed out - republican air forces subsequently attacked Toledo, Talavera, Cáceres, and several other towns. Such activity was not pursued by the Republic on the scale soon adopted by German and Italian units operating on the nationalist side. Nonetheless, it could be argued that the innocent citizens of Guernica had reaped a whirlwind from a wind sown by others. At all events, this correspondence-column exchange of ex-combatants proved to be the last public skirmish on the Cardiff front of the Spanish Civil War.

The final whimper of Welsh resistance to Franco was heard in Penarth. As if to prove the old adage that 'What Penarth does today, the rest of Wales will do tomorrow', a meeting was arranged in the local library on 8th February, 1939, in order to set up a Committee for Spanish Relief. The main instigator was Miss K. Hughes, the energetically philanthropic headmistress of the County Girls School in the town. She announced that their work would be 'non-political and non-sectarian'[39], and that a start had already been made on a fund, with each girl in the school contributing one-half-penny per week. 'Later in the evening', the report added, 'a committee was formed to arrange for a food ship to go from Penarth to take provisions for the suffering Spanish people'[39]. Time was running out for this expedition. Catalonia had already been overrun by the Nationalists. In late March 1939, resistance in Madrid at last crumbled and nationalist forces entered the city. On April 1st General Franco announced that the war was over.

Chapter Three: Cardiff to Odessa via Valencia

Of Marriages and Mutinies

Hardly had Fr. Hannon settled in Aberavon as its new parish priest in September 1936, than he returned to Cardiff in order to officiate at an event which represented at least one happy outcome of the situation in Spain:

> Through the revolt in Spain, a Spanish ship's engineer, Juan Echevarría, came to Cardiff, where he met Señorita Josephina Avilez, daughter of a well -known Spanish family in Cardiff ... When the Spanish ship's crew refused to sail for Sharpness, alleging that the officers carried munitions of war, the officers were unemployed until orders arrived. Juan Echevarría received notification he could remain for three months.... They were married on September 24.[40]

In other respects, however, the ramifications of the situation in Cardiff Docks were more menacing. In the House of Commons, a Home Office spokesman, replying to a question from the communist M.P., Willie Gallagher, explained why the crew of the S.S. *Conde de Abasolo*, which docked at Cardiff in November, had been denied shore leave. 'Police reported that the two men named [Enrique Aparicio, a wireless operator and fireman Manuel Matios], had been making threats against the lives of other Spaniards in Cardiff.'[41] The immigration officer, B.E. Reeve-Jones, felt it advisable to withdraw leave for the whole ship, whilst Matíos was quickly transferred to another vessel bound for Argentina. It is possible that this incident (in spite of the M.P.'s obvious suspicions) was a private matter, and had no political implications - though it obviously involved members of the Spanish community. Indeed, other evidence indicates, in the wake of the bad feeling engendered by the seamen's strike earlier that year, that a kind of civil war in miniature existed, whether overtly or covertly, on board most of the ships of the Spanish merchant marine. At the end of the year, two Spanish ship's officers, Ramón Bengoechia and Eduardo Artelo, arrived in Cardiff having fled from a steamer in the port of Hull. Police had boarded the *Andutz Mendi* and discovered 'a great deal of communistic literature' which they obliged the officers to destroy. At a court hearing in Cardiff where the men, who came to contact the shipping agents, were charged with illegal immigration, their counsel pleaded that

> There was a small Soviet on board the ship and the crew threatened the officers.... If this ship had gone back to sea with the officers on

> board they would most certainly have been in peril of their lives ... The police are asking if means can be found to take these men back to Bilbao ... where there is home rule. There they will be safe. The brother of Bengoechia holds an important position in the Basque Government.[42]

This situation represented a much smaller version of an earlier pattern of events involving the Spanish Navy. In July 1936, around one-half of the warships in the Spanish fleet had been taken over by their crews, after the officers refused to obey Madrid's orders to impede the passage of Franco's army across the straits of Gibraltar. Many officers were literally strung up from their own yard-arms, or else thrown overboard. However, although the mutiny denied the rebels possession of the bulk of the fleet, it brought little advantage to the government. These warships were thereafter mostly confined to port whilst virtually a whole new officer class was trained and commissioned. By the time that Prieto, as navy minister, had restored the fleet's battleworthiness, the Italians, Franco's allies, had taken over Majorca and made it a major naval base for operations against the Republic, for good measure turning the island into a jumbo-sized aircraft carrier. Traffic from the Soviet Union, the government's lifeline as far as military supplies were concerned, began to come under attack. But already by the winter of 1936-7, the rebels having occupied much of Spain's richest food-growing and stock-raising territory, the loyalist zone was short of food. Moreover, a number of important naval vessels based in the west - Cadiz, La Coruña, and El Ferrol - had been acquired by the Nationalists, who thus were able to gain commmand of the waters of the western and northern coasts.

During the summer of 1937, after a year of war, the nationalist armies, aided by the Italian expeditionary force of so-called 'Black Arrows', gradually overcame the resistance of Spain's northern provinces, thus eliminating a large-scale pocket of pro-Republican support and successfully closing a major front. The loss of the Basque country meant that much heavy industrial capacity was lost to the Republic and swung the economic balance decisively against them. Amongst other things, Franco's capture of Bilbao on 19th June threatened the Republic with the outright loss of the greater part of its merchant marine, since the owners of ships registered there would now be obliged (in most cases, with relief) to transfer their enterprises to the nationalist interest. In a desperate attempt to preserve its lifelines with European ports which provided food supplies, the Valencia government issued a decree expropriating all Spanish-registered merchant shipping. The action applied to over seventy vessels, many of which were in British waters or harbours - including a number at Cardiff and Barry.

The Valencia decree generated considerable controversy and incident. On 7th July, three Royal Navy destroyers quitted Cardiff after an official visit - a departure which perhaps was soon to be seen as badly-timed by some. In the second week of July 1937, four Spanish ships came in to various berths. The *Cristina* (1,300 tons) berthed at Roath Dock on 8th and was followed by the *Santurce* (1,900) at Bute East on 10th and the *Marqués de Urquijo* (1,600) at Queen Alexandra on 13th. At this point, the *Astoi Mendi* was apparently already loading. In Barry, the *Marte* and the *Abondi Mendi* were also already loading, the former with coal (ostensibly) for Argentina. All six vessels were owned by Bilbao-based companies which had enjoyed longstanding relationships with commercial partners in South Wales.

The *Cristina*, which had brought in a cargo of pitprops, became the focus of the whole affair. On 14th July the *Western Mail* reported:

> The crew of the Spanish steamer Cristina lying at Cardiff Docks were involved in an incident on Tuesday.... It is alleged that the crew, who are all supporters of the Spanish government, put the captain, chief engineer, second mate and other officers ashore ... contending that they were Fascists and were planning to sail the vessel to Bilbao upon completion of discharge to hand her over to Franco's representatives. The crew have drawn up the gangway and refused to allow anyone on board, so that unloading operations were brought to a standstill. The captain conducted negotiations from the quayside through the first officer who still remained on board acting as intermediary.[43]

The ships' owners took out injunctions and filed suits against the crew and the Republic, but this had little effect on the ground. The main lead in the drama was now taken by Spanish consul in Cardiff, Señor Clemente Cebada, who also harangued the crews from the quayside - but in this case, in order to stiffen resistance to their captain! The immigration officer, Reeve-Jones, claimed that the consul had successfully 'incited' the crews to mutiny against officers and owners, and confirmed that hands aboard *Cristina* were 'of the opinion that the master and chief engineer are fascists and have ejected them'[44]. In Barry, however, the opposite situation prevailed. When the consul, accompanied by officials from the London embassy, went aboard the *Marte*, the skipper, true to the spirit of his ship's name (i.e. Mars, the God of War) refused to surrender his command, and simply ignored notice of dismissal by the Republican government. Mr Reeve-Jones complained to London that Señor Cebada was 'a new consul and extremely undiplomatic. [He] will not discuss matters in a quiet way, but flies into a rage.'[44]

16.
The Fascist leader William Joyce - future 'Lord Haw Haw' - around the time of his visit to Cardiff in 1937.

The whole affair caused consternation in the Foreign Office. A perplexed junior official noted that:

> It seems an extraordinary situation, but it appears to be the case that the police will not interfere in case of mutiny on a foreign ship in British waters, and have no power to assist the owners and the masters.[45]

Though (reading between the lines) this was regarded as a lamentable situation by the authorities, the Foreign Office was bound to advise that no proceedings could be taken against the consul unless his actions could be construed as constituting a breach of the peace on British soil. He had not - as Reeve-Jones claimed - offended against immigration laws, but

> in the present case has done the opposite; he has persuaded the men to refuse to sail and to stay on board the ship so that the owners cannot put a new crew on board.... But whether such action is the sort of thing that is normally within the rights of an accredited consular official is another matter: it certainly looks somewhat odd.[45]

Señor Cebada and the half-dozen crew of the *Cristina* had stumped the British Foreign Office and apparently created an unprecedented dilemma for international law. The little steamship had become a microcosm of the Republic, a symbol of a victory for the people that still might be obtained in Spain. Meanwhile, however, others were planning to breach the peace of Cardiff in a more unequivocal way in order to destroy this symbol. Around this time, William Joyce - later to become notorious as 'Lord Haw-Haw', the pro-Nazi wartime broadcaster - arrived in Grangetown. Earlier that year, Joyce, who had long been Mosley's second-in-command, had split from the B.U.F. in order to set up his own party, the National Socialist League. Joyce advocated a more extreme antisemitic policy than his leader was prepared to contemplate, and one which took a higher profile in identifying British fascism with the major fascist movements on the continent. More particularly, he hoped that a policy of support for Franco would bring him support among Catholic Irish docklands communities - in London, Glasgow and Liverpool as much as in Cardiff. Amongst others, Mosley's propaganda man in South Wales, J. W. O'Neill transferred his allegiance to what soon became known as the 'Brownshirts'. Joyce (who was, of course, himself of Irish origin) stayed with friends at the O'Neill home in Merches Gardens whilst they explored the possibilities of organising a detachment of fascists to march on the *Cristina*, throw out the crew and hand the ship over to the officers - and thus, indirectly, to Franco.

The timing of the whole affair could hardly have been better calculated to excite partisan involvement, on the one hand, and official concern on the other. As we have seen, only days before the confrontation in the docks began, Basque refugee children had arrived in South Wales, to the accompaniment of much newspaper publicity and local emotion. In the wake of the terror-bombing of Guernica, even the staunchly Tory *Western Mail* had perceptibly shifted its sympathies against Franco. The civic authorities, however, were less concerned with the little Bilbaïnos than with more august visitors: the recently-crowned king and queen were due to arrive in Cardiff for their first official visit on 14th July. The prevailing background circumstances demanded even greater guarantees of security and demonstrations of popular loyalty than would normally have been the case. King Edward VIII's recent abdication (December 10th, 1936) had followed hard on the heels of his visit to the South Wales valleys the previous November, during which the king was famously and widely believed to have sympathised with the plight of the Rhondda unemployed, to the extent of expressing private criticism of government policy. The reputation thus gained - whether or not actually deserved - brought him a reciprocal sympathy from the people of South Wales over his own problems with the British 'establishment' in general, and Mr. Stanley Baldwin in particular.

It is little wonder that no further mention of the troubles in the docks was permitted to reach the newspapers (even discounting the sheer priority of space given to the royal visit) until nearly a fortnight after king and queen had been and gone. Then, on 27th July, it was reported that four Spanish ships had been 'arrested' by customs officials, who ceremonially nailed to each mainmast a 'writ of attachment' pending legal decision as a result of the owners' proceedings. 'A representative of the Admiralty Marshall has taken possession

17.
The Spanish steamer Marqués de Urquijo being 'arrested' by an Admiralty official in Cardiff Docks, July 1937.

of each case and has remained on board'[46], the *Western Mail* portentously announced. However at the initial hearing in the High Court of the Admiralty - again centring on the *Cristina* - the counsel retained by the owners, Compañía Naviera Vascongada of Bilbao, succeeded in irritating the judge, who subsequently gave judgement on all four of the Cardiff cases in favour of the legal government of Spain, with costs against the plaintiff. The Spanish Ambassador, Pablo de Azcárate, was jubilant, cabling to Valencia; 'Judgement has great importance since provides precedent for 36 other ships in British waters'[47]. The ambassador's delight proved premature. The owners appealed against the Admiralty Court judgement, and in November the House of Lords agreed to consider the case. Meanwhile, rumours of 'fascist plots' continued to circulate, and the *Western Mail* ran the following:

> A scare story appeared in a London newspaper on Wednesday to the effect that the agents of Gen. Franco and of the Italian Government were planning the violent seizure of the Spanish Government ships lying in the port of Cardiff and their removal to Insurgent forces in Spain. In authoritative quarters the statement was described to the *Western Mail* as 'fantastic, resembling more than anything else a comic-opera plot in a Ruritanian setting'.[48]

As often proves the way with 'authoritative' sources - such as the *Daily Express*, which told its readers almost every day in this period that 'There will be no war' - five months later the show hit the road. The overture began, the cast and chorus of the operetta (or better, the *zarzuela*) 'Cristina' assembled in the wings, and on 8th March, 1938, at approximately 4 p.m. the curtain went up.

> A large posse of Cardiff City Police Officers were rushed to the Queen Alexandra Dock, Cardiff, late on Tuesday afternoon following an alleged attempt by a body of men, said to be Fascist sympathisers, to

**18.
Police guard on the Bilbao steamer Abondi Mendi in Cardiff docks, following the failed attempt at boarding by a fascist gang, March 1938.**

> seize the Spanish steamer Cristina ... shortly before four o'clock the body of men attempted to board the Cristina but their efforts were repelled by the Spanish crew aboard.[49]

If they were hoping to catch their enemies on board the Spanish galleons in their hammocks enjoying a siesta, then the pro-Francoists had miscalculated - though the likelihood is that the gang ('about a score of men') had failed to keep warning of their intentions from filtering through to the ships. Unusual as it is for any show to start with a matinee, this production actually went one better, by opening in two places simultaneously. For Ruritania also came to Port Talbot, where some thirty fascists also failed to strong-arm their way onto Spanish ships. The owner of a lodging-house in Aberavon told reporters that fourteen men - 'mostly alleged to have come from the East End of London'[49] - had stayed on his premises over the weekend, coming in and out at odd hours and giving each other Nazi salutes. 'Patrick Cox, who said he was in charge of the party denied that he was a fascist, and dismissed allegations of a plot'[49].

After hitting this high-spot, the whole imbroglio faded out, and the case subsequently became tied up in appeal and counter-appeal whilst the ships began to rot away at their moorings. Veteran ex-seaman and Butetown poet, Harry 'Shipmate' Cooke, recalled that some time later

> One silent part of the dock housed three Spanish ships seeking refuge from the Spanish Civil War. They had lain at their berths in Cardiff for so long that sea grass and barnacles had taken hold of their underwater plates, and a passing ship's swell would reveal a marine growth akin to a coral reef.[50]

Although the British Courts in this case had upheld the sovereignty of the

Spanish Republic, it was an empty decision, since the ships were unable to leave without qualified officers - and even if this had been possible, there was simply nowhere for them to go. They had no contracts nor any instructions for fresh voyages. Most of the crews were presumably Basque, or from other areas now in Francoist hands. They had declared themselves as committed opponents of the nationalist cause, and would be marked men in Spain after Franco's ultimate victory. Thus the crews eventually gave up and went ashore. Some of them transferred to sign on with non-Spanish ships, or headed off for other ports in order to do so. Like several of their officers, one or two of the several dozen men involved probably ended up by settling down in Cardiff, at least for a time. Indeed, one angry correspondent - perhaps, to judge by his pen-name of 'British Legionaire'[51], inspired by a hidden political agenda - complained to the press in August that unemployed Spanish seamen were receiving handouts (ten bob a week, so it was alleged in the docks) whilst 'Brits' suffered deprivation. As for the *Cristina*, the ship and its companions were very probably confiscated by the British govermnment during the battle of the Atlantic when every ton was needed. The final fate of the boat whose victory over 'fascism' may have been slightly theatrical but was also politically symbolic, is unknown.

19.
Harry Cooke, ex-seaman, local Cardiff writer.

Not Quite Business as Usual

Despite the allegations of 'British Legionaire' the employment prospects of Cardiff seamen had in fact been generally improved by the Spanish War. Several local shipping companies were well-placed to take advantage of the attractive trading terms now offered by both sides in Spain in order to gain food and fuel supplies. One result was that Harry Cooke ended up in Cardiff, after leaving his native Liverpool aged sixteen, in search of a life at sea. There was nothing doing in his native port, or even in London, but 'in the smoke' he heard that South Wales offered at least a chance of a ship, and so he trudged on foot across southern England towards Cardiff and his first voyage. Constant Brothers was the largest of all the Cardiff firms trading to Spain in this period, with a fleet of sixteen ships. They exclusively sailed to ports held by the nationalist side - and apparently, were able to carry on their business with little effective or sustained hindrance at the Cardiff dockside from the activities of the pro-republican campaign. However, much more attention was gained by those who worked for the other side. As a leading historian of the South Wales shipping industry remarks:

20.
J E Emlyn Jones in his Bute Street office in the 1930s. Today these same rooms are occupied by the Butetown History & Arts Centre.

> During the conflict General Franco often complained that a substantial number of the shipping companies based in the United Kingdom which were engaged in trading to Republican Spain had been formed after the confict began, or if in being prior to July 1936, had expended their fleets to take advantage of the situation. There was certainly much in what he said.[52]

Some shipowners were politically sympathetic to the Republic, such as John Emlyn-Jones, a former Liberal M.P. and well-known humanitarian campaigner. An effective speaker, fluent in both Spanish and French, he knew Spain well, from both the personal and commercial standpoints. He repeatedly condemned Franco from public platforms and put his rich experience as a ship's broker at the disposal of the republican side. Other Cardiff shipmen favoured the government side more as a result of hard-headed business calculations. Among these was Frederick Jones, a Tory councillor and owner of the Abbey Line, who commissioned three new steamers in the mid-thirties, at least one of them specifically to take advantage of the new trading conditions in and around Iberia. This was not surprising since, in one voyage from Rotterdam to Alicante, the *Neath Abbey* brought in a profit greater than that which the ship had previously earned its owner in a year's work. Of course the business was neither as lucrative nor as simple as this makes it appear. All ships trading to Spain had to carry a non-intervention official and incurred swingeing extra insurance premiums whilst 'war wages' of double normal rates were due to the crews. Commerce for the main republican zone (that is, other than the northern coast) had to head for the Mediterranean ports; Valencia and even Alicante were within range of the Italian aerodromes on Majorca, and shipping was also vulnerable to submarine attack. As the tempo of this trade increased with the fall of Bilbao and the other northern ports in summer 1937, about a dozen British ships were damaged or sunk. As P.M. Heaton explains:

> These dangers were well-known by South Wales shipowners and seafarers alike, as many had incurred loss or damage and lives had been lost. However, all concerned, crews and owners alike, decided to continue in the trade, feeling that the risks involved were worth taking. Frederick Jones's masters tended to hug the Spanish coast when proceeding to and from the straits of Gibraltar, and had one or two narrow squeaks.[53]

Hugging the coast was not always a good idea. Once inside Spanish territorial waters any vessel on republican business was subject to the attentions of the nationalist navy and even more exposed to those of their air-forces. As late as March 1939, the seventeen-year-old Harry Cooke was a deck hand on board the S.S. *Bellwyn* which sailed to Valencia with a cargo of second-hand clothes and tinned food. The coincidence of date suggests that this may have been the consignment (mentioned above) collected by the recently-established Aid Committee in Penarth. The city of Valencia, the republican capital, was by now in effect one great refugee camp swarming with people who had fled before the final, victorious nationalist advance from west to east of the peninsula. Harry recalls hearing heavy gunfire in the distance, as the enemy overcame the last-ditch resistance of the port of Sagunto, less than thirty kilometres to the north. Panic was growing among many who feared reprisals, a tense situation not alleviated by constant air-raids. Returning to Cardiff with a cargo of oranges, the *Bellwyn* was intercepted by nationalist naval vessels off Cape San Antonio - just north of Benidorm. Luckily, they were accompanied by a larger British ship, which drew the Spaniards' attention, and the Welsh skipper took a chance, making a break for it and refusing to heave-to despite two warning shots. Doubtless, at this late stage, and with the war obviously won, the question of the Republic receiving supplies was one of diminished urgency, and Franco's warships probably had orders not to press these situations to a finish. At any rate, the *Bellwyn* made good its escape, and Harry Cooke and his shipmates got back to Cardiff safely and on schedule.

Others were not so fortunate. Some Welsh mariners were forced to undergo the humiliation of boarding and examination on the high seas. Peter Thompson (also seventeen) was on board the *Magdalena*, commanded by his father, Captain

James Thompson of Llandaff, when the ship encountered a nationalist warship some twenty miles off Santander. After resisting the pressure of no fewer than six successive warning shots, Captain Thompson felt that honour was satisfied, and hove-to but, as things turned out, the Spanish search party found nothing suspicious on board. But by this time there had already been civilian deaths as a result of the risks taken by British commerce. In January 1937, an air raid on Tarragona killed seven crewmen of the Grimsby steamer *Thorpeness*, including a Mr. A. Perrott from Barry. The Cardiff-based *Candleston Castle*, which had already been impounded once by the Nationalists, was damaged during a raid on Barcelona in 1938. Stanley Evans, notable as sailor and academic, who lived in Penarth for many years, was Chief Officer on board the S.S. *Philipp M* during a similar attack on the Catalan capital, in which the vessel narrowly escaped. Later that year a film, jointly produced by the National Union of Seaman and the Committee of British shipowners Trading to Spain, dealing with attacks on British Shipping by pro-Franco forces, was confiscated by the Film Censors' Office. 'In the film', reported *The Seaman*, 'strong comments are made about the attitude of the British Government and Mr. Chamberlain is accused of being the first Premier not to give protection to British ships'[54]. The film alleged that as a result of Spanish Nationalist or allied Italian action in Mediterranean waters, twenty British ships had been sunk, and that no fewer than forty sailors had lost their lives.

In this context it seems that South Wales skippers, despite often sharing their surname with the unluckiest sailor in the lore of the sea - the legendary 'Davy Jones' - on the whole achieved a remarkable escape record. It was again the *Neath Abbey* which made the most daring of all the voyages made by British ships during the war. In early 1938, another Captain Jones and his crew sailed the whole length of the Mediterranean and more, from Almería to Odessa. They somehow managed to get back to Valencia carrying invaluable Russian supplies, and avoiding detection by the enemy - despite the fact that by now the western Mediterranean was so risky for pro-republican shipping that the Russian merchant marine itself had been forced to abandon its direct involvement in food supply to Spain. Later that year, the S.S. *Marconi*, coming into Barry with hull and superstructure spattered with shrapnel marks - incurred whilst discharging at Valencia during an air raid - brought home to many locals the fearful reality of modern warfare. Even more hazardous was the clandestine private arms trade itself, based mostly in Marseilles. Before settling in Cardiff during the Second World War, Crete-born Emanuel

Drakakis, a strong communist and stalwart of the Greek seamen's union, took part in several such voyages from France back and forth to Barcelona and Valencia, running the gauntlet of Italian bombers and submarines.

Fifi Calls Franco's Bluff

In the spring of 1937, the predicament of besieged Bilbao became the focus of attention in much of the world's press. The Basque government offered shipping companies tempting premiums for food deliveries, but in reply Franco's navy threatened to sink any ship which dared to run their blockade. It was the celebrated skipper David Jones - 'Potato Jones' or 'el Patatero' - in the Cardiff-registered *Marie Llewellyn* who tried first. Much to his humiliation and disgust, the attempt failed when he was turned back by the Royal Navy. This particular Jones went one better than Davy by becoming a legend in his own lifetime. His name still evokes a reaction in certain maritime quarters, where some regard him as a humanitarian 'Pimpernel', committed to saving lives, whereas others insist he was a profiteer and even a gun-runner. In his indispensable history of the Spanish Civil War, Hugh Thomas states unequivocally that Jones' ostensible cargo was a thin covering for a more deadly payload (which was eventually delivered to Valencia). Nevertheless, the irresistible nickname even reached the offices of the literary journal, the *Left Review*, whose editor, Edgell Rickword, referred to it in the poem (already quoted from) 'To the Wife of any Non-Intervention Statesman':

Restive, our sailors watched the shore
Whilst hundreds drowned who'd starved before,
Victims of Franco's sham blockade -
Though in the way of honest trade
Potato Jones and his brave lass
Had proved this husband knave or ass.

However, Rickword was mistaken about the identities of the blockade-busters. In the meantime, several other 'Jones boys' - both actual and honorary - were lurking in the French port of St. Jean de Luz. These skippers had food cargoes which were threatening to spoil, but the nationalist fleet was on full alert, and the Admiralty in London accepted the Francoist claim that the approaches to the estuary of Bilbao were heavily mined. Then, on April 19th, Captain W.H. Roberts in the Cardiff- registered *Seven Seas Spray* weighed anchor under cover

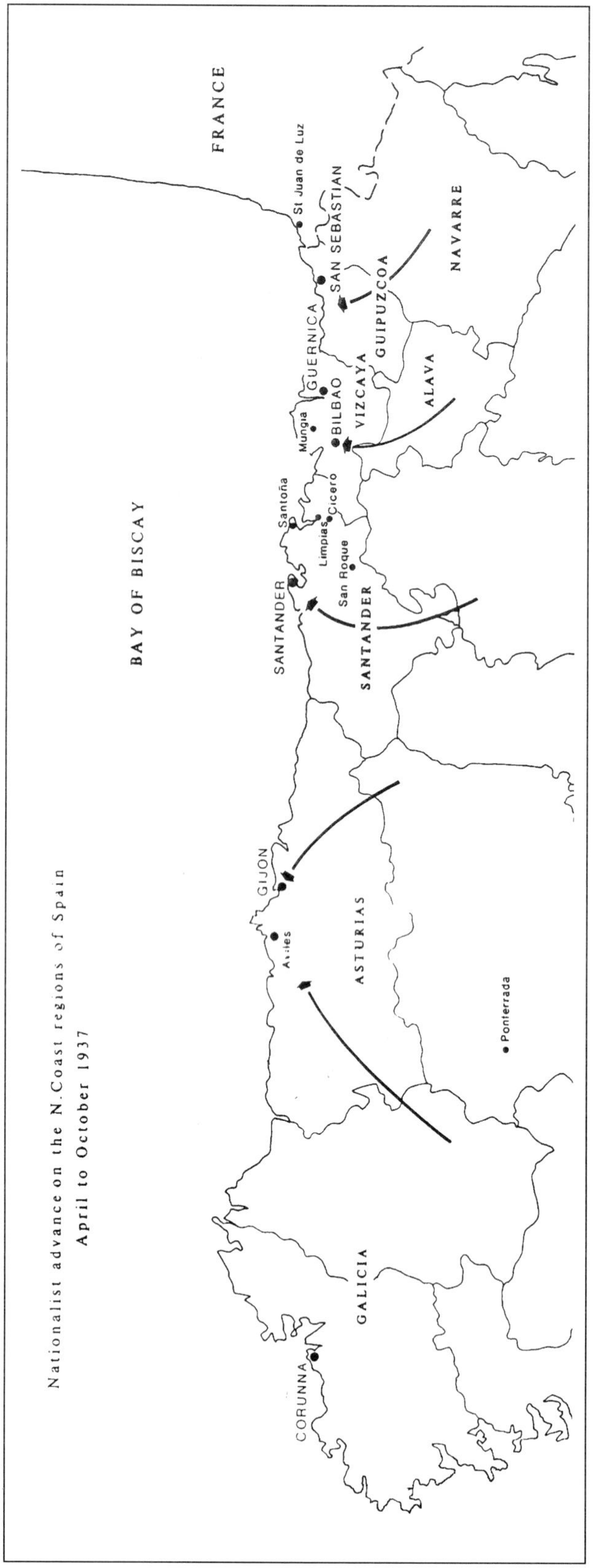

Map 3.
Northern regions of Spain, showing the general thrust of nationalist advances, April-October, 1937.

of darkness and headed straight for Bilbao, where he docked without incident the following morning. There was undoubtedly a good deal of what would today be called 'hype' in skipper Roberts' action. Both he and the ship's owner, Alfred Pope of Porthcawl, were swashbuckling types, and they took maximum advantage of the publicity angle of events. The exploit of the *Seven Seas Spray* made headlines and news bulletins all over the world. Reporters were naturally intrigued by the fact that Roberts' equally adventurous teenage daughter, Fifi, was on board. Apparently unknown to the poet himself, she was Rickword's 'brave lass'. As she wrote to her ex-teachers in Penarth:

> On Monday night 10 p.m. April 19th we slipped out of the bay of St. Jean de Luz, and steamed along with no lights. Dad was up all night, and we got to Bilbao safely. The pirate ship 'Almirante Cervera' was looking the wrong way for once. There's about eight miles of very narrow river to Bilbao from the entrance to Portugalete. On either side of the river people poured out to cheer us, and children shouted 'Vino!' - our foredeck was full of barrels of wine. It was a wonderful welcome, and to me a very touching one. From the day we docked, April 20th, till today we haven't had much peace. On the afternoon of the 20th we went to Durango, which was heavily bombed some time ago. A banquet was held for us on 21st by the Engkadi [Basque] Government, and Dad was presented with an inscribed silver cigarette case, and I, although I had done nothing, with a gold bracelet with the Basque Women's Flag on it.[55]

In a T.V. documentary interview years later, Fifi referred to the ship's dash across the narrow stretch of Biscay as 'father doing his Nelson act - he just shut one eye. When we got to Bilbao we received a ticker-tape reception'[56]. Indeed, the event provided not only real relief but also a propaganda fiesta for the Republic. Under the spotlight of the world's press, Franco's bluff had been called, and his fleet exposed as incompetent. Father and daughter were the heroes of the hour in Bilbao, feted, feasted, filmed and photographed everywhere they went. Moreover, during her ten-day stay in the Basque capital Fifi Roberts acted as a special ace reporter for the pro-republican *News Chronicle*. She herself was a keen photographer. As befitted her new profession she was at supper with the *Times* reporter when a message came through that Guernica had been bombed and was in flames. They were driven to the ancient capital only the day after the Condor Legion had destroyed it, and Fifi, with her camera, duly recorded the scenes of devastation for posterity. Indeed, it is tempting to speculate that the German decision to terror-bomb Guernica may have been an act of vengeance, influenced by the publicity disaster which

21.
'Fifi' Roberts at the height of her fame, being feted in Bilbao, April 1937.

22.
Captain William Roberts on the bridge of the Seven Seas Spray.

the Roberts family and the *Seven Seas Spray* had given the Francoist cause. If so, it was a typically extreme and counter-productive reaction.

Captain Roberts himself was of Cornish origin but he had lived for some years in Penarth. As it happened, only a few weeks before these events took place, the girls of the local High School, where his daughter had been educated, had adopted the *Seven Seas Spray* through a national scheme to encourage interest in maritime matters. In one sense, the fame of the action was well deserved. Alfred Pope told reporters:

> I knew it could be done. My steamer has shown that Franco's blockade is nothing but boast and tommy rot. A British steamer has opened the way for shipping. I hope that the *Spray* has blazed a trail...[57]

Given his character and methods, it is tempting to speculate that Pope had gone out of his way to obtain the patronage of the Penarth School for his ship in advance, conscious of the fact that Lord Plymouth was the local squire. What is more, the earl's father had been virtual founder of the Penarth Secondary Schools, with a generous bequest some forty years earlier; even today the school's symbol incorparates the Plymouth arms. Unfortunately, perhaps, the opinion of the supreme 'non-intervention statesman' himself about this bizarre act of defiance on his own doorstep is not recorded.

23.
The smoking ruins of Guernica after the Condor Legion raid.

The Great Escape

As Alfred Pope foresaw, many other supply-ships reached Bilbao in the wake of the *Seven Seas Spray*. The British government was in deep water: the crisis had caused continuous uproar in Parliament for a week leading up to the *Spray's* voyage. On the advice of both Admiralty and Foreign Office, ministers had repeatedly insisted that Franco's blockade was a reality, and now they had to retract in humiliation. Yet whilst food relief may have alleviated suffering amongst Bilbao's vulnerable citizens, it made no difference to the military situation, as the nationalist forces advanced inexorably. Soon, Welsh steamers were hovering around Bilbao not in the attempt to deliver supplies but in order to pick up human cargoes. The month of June witnessed an intensive improvised ferry service in operation as crowded vessels slipped across to France with refugees. This somewhat grim - if for many potential victims, lifesaving - trade continued throughout much of that summer of 1937. It was only the scene of the action which shifted, along the coastline, as the other ports to the west of Bilbao were besieged and captured - Santander, Santoña, Gijón, and finally Avilés in October. On July 22nd, the Cardiff-based S.S. *MacGregor,* skippered by Captain Owen Jones of Canton, was intercepted by the *Almirante Cervera* which fired no fewer than four times across her bows. Captain Jones, carrying over 2,000 refugees and mindful of the potential fate of many if he surrendered, decided to stick to his course. Thankfully, whatever his orders (and human feelings), the Spanish naval commander was unwilling to add another unfavourable chapter to the recent history of nationalist propaganda disasters - above all, the unprecedented atrocity of Guernica, which had caused Franco to forfeit so much international support.

In the middle of July, the *Western Mail* carried the news that what 'Potato' Jones had bitterly referred to as an Armada of 'Spanish Dons strutting about the quarter-decks of their miserable ships'[58], had at last managed to collar one of the Welsh sea-dogs:

> The Cardiff Steamer Molton (3,091 tons) was captured on Wednesday by the Nationalist cruiser Almirante Cervera inside territorial waters at a point off Santander ... Practically all the firemen and deck hands are coloured men residing in the Cardiff Docks area ... The vessel is one of the local boats that are on time-charter with the Spanish government and left Cardiff about six weeks ago.[59]

This incident also caused a stir in the House of Commons, where members from both sides expressed concern at the apparent inactivity of the nearby H.M.S. *Royal Oak*. Many people inside and outside the House were highly sensitive, for inherited cultural reasons, to any (real or imagined) challenge to British maritime supremacy - especially from Spaniards. Few, however, appreciated the difficult complexities of the legal situation obtaining during a civil war with such a rapidly-changing strategic scenario. Alice Stear, wife of the *Molton*'s commander, alleged to the *South Wales Echo* that her husband was 'a marked man'[60] in Burgos for having been so committed to the rescue of republican refugees. In the event, pressure applied through diplomatic channels procured the rapid release of both the *Molton* and another Cardiff steamer (the *Candleston Castle*) detained whilst pursuing a similar mission. Worse was to come, however, when the now-famous *Seven Seas Spray* itself - despite the support of Penarth County School for Girls - was captured in the port of Santoña when it fell to Italian forces on 25th August. In what was undoubtedly an act of *venganza* for their earlier exploit, Captain Roberts - a 'marked man' if ever there was one - along with his crew and ship were held for over two months in increasingly uncomfortable conditions. Franco turned his own 'blind eye' to Foreign Office enquiries about the *Spray*, whilst granting virtually all other captured ships a more-or-less speedy amnesty.

During this confused and dramatic period, South Wales steamers, Cardiff-owned or Cardiff-based vessels prominent among them, took off thousands of desperate men, women and children - perhaps more than 10,000 in all. In doing so they undoubtedly saved hundreds of lives which may have been at risk in the uncontrolled situation which so often reigned in the immediate aftermath of defeat. The vast majority of those who sought immediate refuge in France returned to Spain within the year - some to make their peace with the new regime as best they could; others, the younger and especially the single men, crossing back into what was left of republican Spain in order to carry on the struggle on another front. But, for all the emotion now being felt, both by participants on the spot and those interested and concerned back home, the fact remained that the whole business was still business. The refugee rescue operation brought in its due and proper profits to those who took financial and physical risks. There may even have been some cynically opportunist privateering. P.M. Heaton, for example, strongly implies that even at the height of the Basque crisis, some cargoes intended for Bilbao fell into nationalist hands by prior arrangement.

24.
Refugees leaving Gijón harbour on the day the port fell to Franco, 21 October, 1937.

Nevertheless, several companies did suffer certain (predictable) consequences of their commitment. Within a few short weeks of the fall of Bilbao and the extinction of the infant Republic of Euskadi, Cardiff's traditional commercial links with the Basque country were renewed, this time on behalf of the new military dictatorship. Whilst Cardiff's mercy-ships ran the gauntlet into Santander and Gijón, steamers of the Constant Brothers' fleet, under the auspices of the new regime, were already loading iron ore in Bilbao docks for the East Moors steel mills. In South Wales, as in the rest of Britain, the tempo of rearmament was beginning to pick up: Spanish raw materials simply could not be overlooked as the situation in Europe became ever more menacing. But Franco made certain that the pro-republican shipowners, like John Emlyn-Jones, Lord Glanely and Alfred Pope, could wave goodbye to any further Spanish contracts. Especially given the remarks made above about business interest, it must also be stated that, in some cases, this was the cause of serious economic loss to the businessmen concerned. Indeed, it is said that, following years of depression, more than one Cardiff shipman was finally ruined by support for the Spanish Republic. This represents a tangible sacrifice for a cause in which they believed. It was made by men (and by their families) whose material circumstances may have been considerably better than those of the working class with whom - in this context - we normally associate the word 'sacrifice'. Such people were not of the 'orthodox' pro-Republican lobby, but their suffering is not for that reason less worthy of record.

25.
Luis Cicero in the 1930s.

Chapter Four: Testaments of War

So far, this book has been confined to a generally abstract analysis of the effects of the Spanish Civil War on Cardiff and, via a kind of reciprocation, of Cardiff's maritime involvement with the war. These have been illustrated by the reconstruction of incidents and the re-telling of stories which involved individual protaganists or witnesses. The people and communities concerned were influenced by the war to a greater or lesser degree. To many, it represented little more than a passing phase in their lives, but there were (and are) other individuals and families whose lives were utterly changed by the experience of the war. Lives were transformed through emotional identification with the cause of one side, direct participation in the fighting itself, or (in one case) by its dynamic, if indirect, impact on the development of an intellectual personality and successful writer. Some of these stories are striking in themselves by the quality of conviction or the intensity of experience they embody. Others impress more by their typicality or topicality to the era, that is, they reflect towards us some recognised characteristics of the 1930s generation. All of them illuminate not only the continuing meaning that memories of the Spanish war has for individuals, and their families and friends, who live in today's Cardiff but also the searing effect of political and personal emotions evoked by those memories. These emotions are attested by the fact that, occasionally, some wounds can be somewhat tender to the touch even after the healing effect of sixty years.

Cardiff Spaniards at War

The oldest surviving Cardiff veteran of the Spanish War, Luis Cicero, is an exception to nearly all the general observations made so far, for he became an adoptive Cardiffian only in 1940, after the Spanish War was over. Some time around 1930, as a young man looking for work, he moved to the city of Santander from his home village of Cicero, some forty kilometres distant. He was lucky enough to get a job as a tram-conductor in the busy commercial-naval port. As a child, his politically radical father had refused to bring him up as a practising Catholic, and once established in Santander he moved naturally towards support for socialism and membership of the U.G.T. In July 1936, when news of the military rising reached Santander, he enlisted in the Union's militia. A year later, as Franco's forces resumed their westward advance along the coast after the fall of Bilbao, his unit was gradually forced back towards Santander. He remembers the sight of advancing Italians and Moorish units from positions in the hills to the east of the city. By now Cicero had risen to the rank of captain, but he realised that, given the strength of the 'fifth column' in his rear, Santander was impossible to defend.

The Cardiff steamer *Pilton*, one of Lord Glanely's line, was in Santander during the days immediately before its fall. The chief engineer on board later recorded a harrowing eyewitness description of the apocalyptic atmosphere which prevailed.

> When we got alongside the wharf we soon became aware that we were in a doomed town ... Children clustered at the foot of the gangplank in the hope that someone would throw them a piece of bread ... The children who roamed the waterfront were orphans of the war ... There was no-one to take up the task of looking after their welfare, so they formed into packs, hunted about for what food they could get and at night slept on the beach. Into the town itself there drifted a never-ending stream of refugees from Bilbao and the surrounding countryside ... the schools, churches and public buildings were already full of wounded soldiers and refugees ... At night the quayside was lit by innumerable small fires around which destitute families clustered for warmth ... The distant rumble of gunfire became louder ... Spies were everywhere, friend and foe mixed not knowing one another ... Men worked feverishly in the town square preparing dug-outs while long queues of women waited outside shops with their ration cards, and over the whole scene the painted ladies smiled wickedly down from their balconies, ready to welcome the oncoming conquerors.[61]

Luis Cicero's unit retreated on Santoña, a town situated on a small peninsula, and soon cut off by Italian motorised forces. He was very fortunate in this circumstance, since the Italians were disinterested in the dubious pleasure of reprisals and tended - for a time at least - to overlook the evacuation of refugees. Cicero was fearful, knowing that his life, as an officer and known socialist, may well have been forfeit in the event of capture. In a stroke of luck, he managed to find a small local fishing boat which took him across to France. He landed at Le Havre and went on to Paris, where he contacted the pro-republican organisations. Like thousands of others who had escaped from the shambles of northern Spain, he was determined to return to the fight.

Before the end of 1937, he reached Barcelona by sea from Marseilles and enlisted once more in the loyalist army. From Barcelona he was sent to the most distant part of the front - the Sierra Morena - to guard the mercury mines of Almadén. This major mineral-extraction complex represented the largest mercury source in Europe, and was of great interest to Franco's German and Italian allies as a highly-prized strategic material. This was the reason why, on the one hand, it was so heavily defended by the Republic, and why on the other, it never in the event suffered a heavy nationalist attack likely to damage its installations. After the collapse of the Extremadura front consequent upon the failure of General Rojo's republican offensive in late 1938, Luis was caught up in the long retreat to the Mediterranean. In March 1939, he managed to reach Alicante. There he tried once again to obtain a passage to safety; but this time he was not so lucky. As the victorious Nationalists approached, he and his compadres decided it was better to die in their own *pueblos* than in distant Alicante. Three friends - Cicero, a fellow *Santanderino*, and an Asturian ex-miner - got out of the town and headed north on a long trek across country. They travelled only by night, holing up by day in cattle sheds or abandoned homesteads (a feature of the landscape which the war had considerably increased).

The men somehow managed to reach Bilbao, where Cicero stowed away on a ship bound for Halifax, Nova Scotia. Arriving in Canada, he had no papers and did not know one word of English. In effect without statehood or identity, he was forced into the only feasible existence - he became a sailor. His induction to the life was almost fatal. In early 1940 Cicero was on board a Canadian supply ship which was attacked and sunk by German planes 200 miles out of Glasgow. He was picked up by a lifeboat and taken to Greenock. Thereafter, he tried to jump ship in Britain several times, but was always interned as an enemy alien. However, when the same happened in Cardiff, the local branch of the International Brigade Association, hearing that he had fought with the Republic, intervened and managed to procure both his release and a visa. For some months, he went to stay in the Esplanade Hotel, Penarth, maintained at the cost of the I.B.A. One day, he went looking for a job with a Spanish contact, who was lodging in the house where Mary Sanchez lived in Luisa Street. According to Mary, he arrived as a big air raid was starting - possibly one of the major attacks of January, 1941. Shortly thereafter, Luis and Maria were married. As an alien, Cicero had to report to the police on a daily basis, but the couple were given work by the Miners' Union in Cardiff, helping out in their offices in Windsor Place.

Given his record of hair-raising escapes, it seems that Luis Cicero was also fortunate that he never got back to his home village in 1939, for there and then he almost certainly would have ended his days. About seventeen people known for republican affiliations were executed in the town, and Luis' own brother was imprisoned in the notorious prison of Dueso (in Santoña) for twelve years. His family were thrown on to the street to fend for themselves, and their home allocated to supporters of the victorious side. About a year after Franco's death in 1975, Cicero returned to his village and confronted the occupant of his old home - who stood his ground and claimed to have acquired the property quite legally.

As we have already seen, José María ('Joe') Larreta Lotina was born in the heart of Tiger Bay - to be precise, in Loudoun Square - in April 1916. After the family returned to Spain because of his mother's terminal illness, his father ran a ferry boat on the Ria de Mundaka, in northern Vizcaya (also sometimes called 'Ria de Gernika') operating from the beach of Laida, opposite the town of Mundaka itself. The place is one of surpassing natural beauty, which even in those days attracted many tourists. José Larreta worked on the ferry in his school holidays. At eighteen, he went to college in Bilbao, hoping to become an engineer, but was forced to give up the course when the death of his father obliged him to help support his brothers and sisters. His father had influenced him in favour of socialism; Señor Larreta senior subscribed to the P.S.O.E. newspaper and possessed a small library of radical books. Lacking a mother, the children were not brought up to be religious, and Catholicism meant little or nothing to young José when growing up. He spoke some Basque with his playmates - or a mixture of Basque and Spanish - but did not read or write Euskara, and was disinterested in the cause of 'national' separatism. On the other hand, he remembers being deeply moved by the Asturias rising and its fate, events which happened when he was a student in 1934. Broadly speaking, he regarded himself as a supporter of Indalecio Prieto's moderate wing of the Socialist Party.

26.
Joe Larreta in the early 1940s.

In July 1936, José Larreta answered the party call and headed for San Sebastian, the town nearest to the rebels who were based in Navarre. Here the Basque people's army was being assembled for an offensive. He took his father's shotgun and a haversack loaded with sticks of dynamite - in imitation of his Asturian coalminer heroes of the 1934 uprising. But it was the enemy leader, Mola who dealt the first blow, and the defence of Guipúzcoa collapsed rapidly.

After retreating to Bilbao, Larreta was assigned to a machine gun battalion. Later that year, he and his comrades were sent to occupy the heights overlooking Vitoria - capital of the tiny Basque province of Alava which was a nationalist stronghold. After six freezing weeks, they were relieved, and following a period of leave, occupied another front, guarding a vital pass into the coastal plain. He was based at Archanda on the heights of Bilbao when the city fell (June 1937) and the Basque army retreated west into Cantabria. Not long afterwards, he was taking part in operations high in the mountains, against the town of San Roque de Riomiera, when he contracted typhoid fever. He was evacuated to a hospital at Limpias - not far from Cicero, the home *pueblo* of Luis.

Only partially recovered, as the enemy advanced he was sent to a hospital near Gijón (Asturias) to convalesce. It was only a brief respite, and by the autumn, Gijón too was threatened. Though the town (unlike Santander) was thoroughly republican, the strength of its defenders had been sapped by the prolonged resistance of the local military barracks, and the rebels had been aided by continuous shelling from the nationalist navy. By the autumn, defensive operations were virtually paralysed by the constantly rising tide of refugees. Early in the morning of 21st October - the day the enemy entered the town - Larreta managed to get a place on board a refugee boat. It seemed he had escaped a nationalist vengeance which one historian calls 'ferocious'. Not long out of port, however, the rescue boat was intercepted by the nationalist warship *Almirante Cervera*. The cruiser put a complement on board, and it was taken into Santoña. This harbour town, situated on a little peninsula guarding a beautiful river estuary, provides a geographical point of coincidence for no fewer than three of our chief subjects. First, it was the very place where, a few weeks earlier, Luis Cicero had experienced somewhat better luck in escaping from his victorious enemies. Second, and more extraordinary, our old shipmate the *Seven Seas Spray* (see above, p. 76) was at this point still impounded, and anchored in Santoña bay. From this vantage point, Fifi Roberts, 'marooned' on board her father's vessel actually witnessed the refugee boat, on which José Larreta and hundreds of others were awaiting their fate, being brought in. She reported the event to her school magazine:

> On 21st - the day of the fall of Gijon - there was a grand procession along the quay. Soldiers from the barracks marched along with civilian men and women and hordes of children, and waved Franco, Fascist, German, Italian and Portuguese flags. Small fishing boats blew their

> hooters, and great was the noise! The next day, all the North coast fell to Franco, and an even grander procession took place along the quay. Fireworks were let off during the evening, and to give the proceedings the right touch, a captured Spanish ship entered port, full of prisoners from Gijon and Asturias.[62]

By this time, of course, the Italians had moved out and Franco's men were in full control. On board his captured ship, José Larreta had had time to think and hit on a cunning plan. When he was taken to be interrogated, he claimed to be British, and a member of the republican ambulance corps (machine gunners were often the objects of severe 'reprisals'). There was no passport or any other shred of proof of the prisoner's assertions - not to mention his total ignorance of English. Not surprisingly, his captors were not wholly convinced - though equally, they may have asked themselves whether anyone could have invented such an unlikely story. But the men on the spot could not afford to risk a mistake. Had they acted summarily, it might have caused a diplomatic incident of embarrassment to Burgos, and they would doubtless have incurred the wrath of the *generalísimo*.

In the meantime, the claim at least meant that Larreta avoided the hell-hole of Dueso. For some months he was confined as a special prisoner in the Santoña barracks. Though he was not aware of it at the time, his fate hung delicately in the balance. Various Francoists who had spent time as holidaymakers in Mundaka had already reported his name to the intelligence authorities as a known socialist and member of the Basque army. His sister, Aurora, was interrogated by Francoist police in the family home. But one connection of theirs was an officer in an elite Navarrese regiment which had taken part (on the nationalist side) in the recent campaign. He interceded for Larreta, whilst Aurora managed to contact the British embassy to Spain, which was now located on neutral territory across the French border in Hendaye. In mid-November, the Nationalist Foreign Ministry in Burgos received a note from Sir Henry Chilton, British Ambassador:

> His Majesty's Embassy present their compliments to the Secretariat of Foreign Affairs and have the honour to state that it has come to their notice that a certain José Maria Larreta, who is alleged to have been born at Cardiff on April 11th 1916, is a prisoner of war at the Instituto de Manzanedo, Carcel del Dueso, Santoña. His Majesty's Embassy would be glad to learn whether the above individual is in fact under detention at the place named and, if so, what charges are pending against him.[63]

27.
'Fifi' Roberts in her element aboard her father's ship.

Despite its non-committal tone, this note probably saved Larreta's life, since Chilton was highly respected in Burgos for his barely-concealed pro-nationalist views. Nevertheless, the Francoists were still unwilling officially to concede the point, sending him to a P.O.W. camp in Miranda del Ebro, where about 6,000 republican captives were held. Late in 1937, he was integrated in a labour battalion and sent to the Teruel front, in the snow-bound mountains of southern Aragon, where the Republic had launched an unexpected - and, at first, successful - attack. Special prisoners were allowed the privilege of being in a work unit, where they were actually paid, at the royal rate of three-quarters of a peseta a day. After a desperate and bloody struggle in sub-zero temperatures, anticipating the horrors of Stalingrad, the town of Teruel was recaptured by the Nationalists in early February, and Larreta and his fatigue were sent in to clear up the streets of the city.

He stayed in Teruel, engaged in the rebuilding of the completely ruined town, until the spring of 1938. Then, it seems, his claim to British nationality was officially accepted and he was sent to the main centre for captured foreigners just outside Burgos. In the prison camp of San Pedro de Cardeña - actually a deconsecrated monastery none too ceremoniously adapted for this purpose - Joe was incarcerated with all the prisoners from the International Brigades.

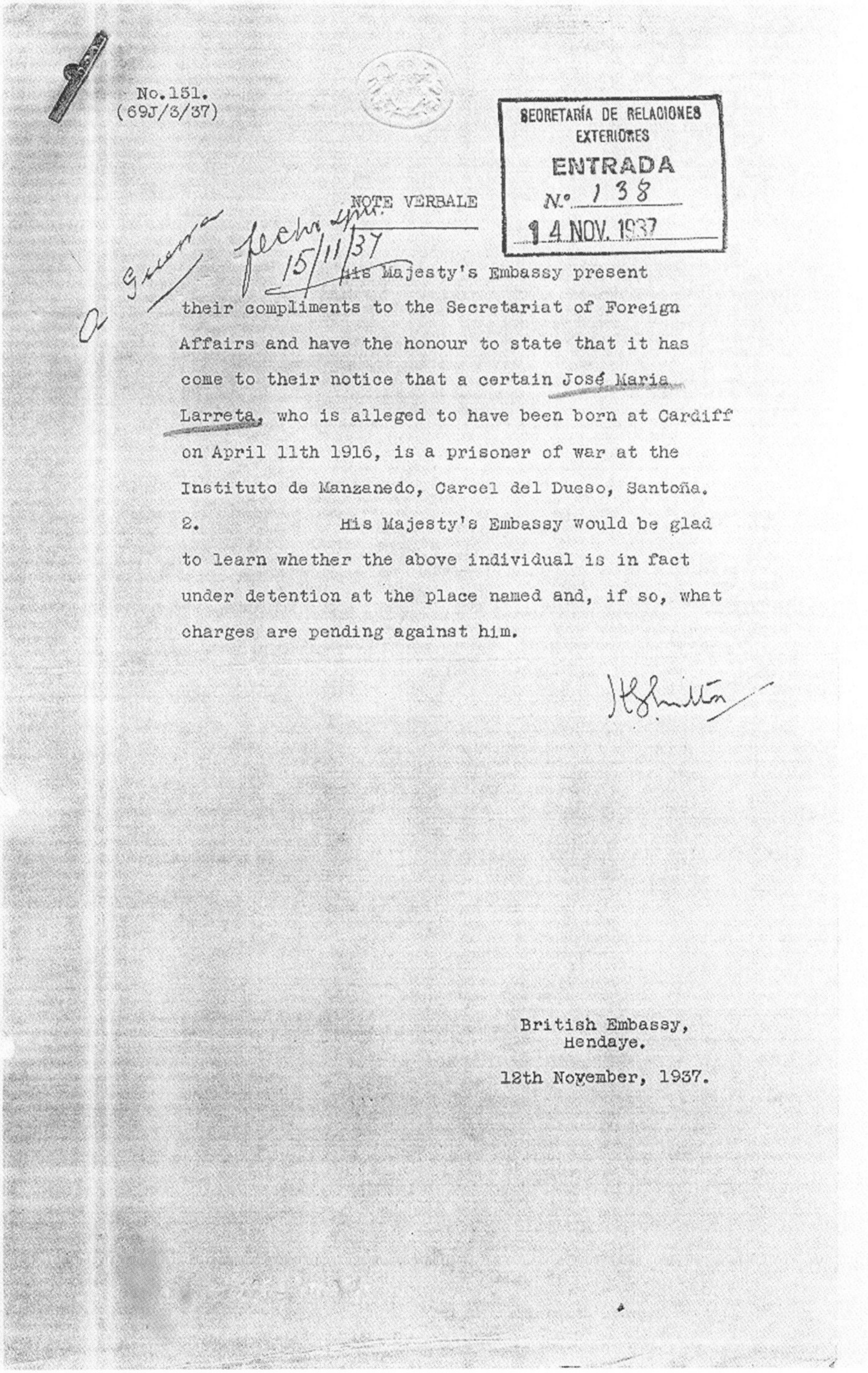

No.151.
(69J/3/37)

SECRETARÍA DE RELACIONES EXTERIORES
ENTRADA
N.° 138
14 NOV. 1937

NOTE VERBALE

a Guerra
fecha 15/11/37

His Majesty's Embassy present their compliments to the Secretariat of Foreign Affairs and have the honour to state that it has come to their notice that a certain José Maria Larreta, who is alleged to have been born at Cardiff on April 11th 1916, is a prisoner of war at the Instituto de Manzanedo, Carcel del Dueso, Santoña.

2. His Majesty's Embassy would be glad to learn whether the above individual is in fact under detention at the place named and, if so, what charges are pending against him.

British Embassy,
Hendaye.

12th November, 1937.

28.
Ambassador Chilton's note to the Nationalist Foreign Office, 1938.

**30.
José María Larreta with a group of compadres (back row, right) - all veterans of the Republican armies - around 1940.**

His name appears as number 38 on a list of British inmates at San Pedro (April 1938), and occurs next to that of another adoptive Cardiffian (Richard Jones, originally North Walian). In the camp Larreta met a prisoner who was in a similar situation to himself - an American national who had been born in Miami but whose Cuban family later moved back to Spain. His compadre possessed an English-Spanish dictionary, and they began to learn English together. They got to know members of the British contingent and were helped especially by Jimmy Moon, a Reading lab technician turned 'camp journalist'. Joe's memories of conditions at San Pedro are by no means idyllic, but are perhaps less grisly than those attested by most International Brigade victims. There were 800 prisoners, housed on two floors of the monastery, with every 200 men sharing three latrines and two taps. The food was meagre and treatment often severe - but falling short of the sadistic. Over time, batches of French, North American and British prisoners were released, whilst those less fortunate (such as the Germans) were taken away to a different fate. By late May 1939, nearly two months after the end of the war, Larreta was amongst the few who had still not gained his freedom. Finally, with what he believed were the last nine Britishers, he was taken to San Sebastian and placed in jail at Hondarreta. A week later, they were taken across the international bridge into France, where the Red Cross were waiting to give them a communal bath. Larreta was then over six foot two in height, and had lost over two stones - looking 'like an old coat-hanger in the passage' as he put it. He was given an old suit much too small for him and - as if to even things up - a pair of boots several sizes too big.

30.
Joe Larreta today with his copy of Picasso's famous 'Guernica'.

On arrival at Newhaven, Larreta was questioned by immigration, but was soon passed through. When his train got to London's Victoria Station, the International Brigade Association representatives were waiting to welcome him. He was taken for a meal and then to a hostel. But after two years of imprisonment, he rebelled against the confining discipline of this billet and was soon in trouble. It was his sister, Aurora, who again came to the rescue. She had written to their old Cardiff neighbours, the Barracaldo family, one of whom was in a position to procure him a job as steward on board a Liverpool cruise liner. His first voyage was to Buenos Aires, and as the liner was crossing the Atlantic, war broke out in Europe. In the River Plate, he vividly remembers the sight of the German heavy cruiser *Graf Spee* lying recently scuttled outside Montevideo harbour. In 1941, Joe Larreta returned to Cardiff, after a twenty-year absence. He spent the rest of the war in the merchant navy and 'retired' to a job in the Mountstuart dry-dock a few years after his marriage in 1947. Though Joe Larreta's basic feelings about politics and the Spanish War have never changed, he is not a bitter man: he felt able to return to the Basque country for a holiday well before Franco's death - as long ago as 1962.

The Internationals - Part One

According to Hywel Francis' book, *Miners Against Fascism*, Cardiff (along with Penarth) contributed seventeen men to fight in Spain as members of the Fifteenth International Brigade. The present research suggests that this may be a slight underestimate (see Appendix 1), though ultimately any figure depends on the criteria applied in its production. Like all the other British volunteers, recruits from the Cardiff area had experiences which can be arranged into four main categories. Of the twenty-five men who qualify by my calculations, it seems that seven were killed or fatally wounded in action; at least five were repatriated (either having been seriously wounded, or on grounds of sickness or compassion); two were captured by the enemy, and spent time in a prison camp; lastly, perhaps as many as nine men were under arms when the Brigades were dissolved in October 1938.

The first Cardiffian to fall was Bill Coles, killed on February 14th, 1937 - truly a St. Valentine's Day Massacre as far as the British Battalion was concerned. This was the third day of the battalion's astonishingly courageous and (as it proved) vital stand against the furious Nationalist onslaught across the Jarama valley, which runs south from Madrid to Aranjuez. Bill Coles was one of over a hundred British comrades to die in this desperate struggle amongst the random terrain of low hills - the Sierra de Pingarrón - to the south of the narrow country road from San Martín de la Vega to Morata de Tajuña. Nothing seems to be known about the immediate circumstances of his death, and only a little about the young life which was thus ended. Bill Coles was born in Splott in or around 1910. His family was working class, and highly active in support of the Labour Party. He himself was called 'Little Bolshie' by friends - the nickname was a typical oxymoron, since he was in fact over six feet tall. Several uncles and brothers were part of the Guest Keen labour force over the years, but leaving school at the start of the depression, Coles failed to find employment. Exploiting his height and physique, he joined the Welsh Guards for a five-year stint. Discharged around 1934, he succeeded this time in getting a job at East Moors. Like many others he began to read about politics, and joined the Communist Party. He often frequented a radical bookshop located on the corner of Park Lane and Queen Street, and was very close to the shop manager, a young teacher called Gwen Jones. One morning in December 1936 (his sister, Nancy, recalls) their mother called him for work: 'I'm not going in today, mam' he replied, 'I'm off to Spain'. Bill Coles' body was buried somewhere on the field of battle, and his only headstone is the memorial erected by the International Brigades Association two years ago in San Martín de la Vega, which stands at the centre of the huge Jarama battlefield. At a memorial service held at the Tabernacl in the Hayes, Paul Robeson was present and sang an elegy to Bill's memory.

31.
Bill Coles, around the time he went to Spain.

32.
A typical hill on the Jarama battlefield.

Later that year, a secular memorial meeting was organised by the Party at which fellow-brigaders Will Paynter and John Williams gave speeches. Those present read Browning's lines printed alongside his obituary.

> *I was ever a fighter so ... one more fight,*
> *The best and the last.*
> *I would hate that death bandaged my eyes, and forebore*
> *And bade me creep past.*
> *No! let me taste the whole of it, like my peers*
> *The heroes of old.*[64]

One of the two Penarthians who enlisted in the International Brigades was also involved at Jarama. Harold Patterson was a foundation member of the British Battalion in the early weeks of 1937, when it was christened the 'Saklatvala' Battalion - after a well-known Indian communist who became M.P. for Battersea. Patterson was a member of the machine-gun company which played a crucial role in halting the thrust of Franco's Legionaries on the Morata road. However, on the second day of the British engagement (13th February) the whole of this company of over thirty men was forced to surrender after being surrounded. Patterson later gave an account of his experiences to the *Penarth Times*. Various aspects of this text indicate that it was compiled in the C.P.G.B. offices in King's Road, London, rather than being the first-hand work of the subject himself. Patterson states that he got a shrapnel wound during the fighting; this forced his retirement from the front, and ultimately his return home. Whilst other details of Patterson's story are convincing, it seems more plausible that he was captured with the rest of his company. This experience (however) was omitted from his published account, the better to preserve morale on the home front by not describing the humiliations of surrender and imprisonment. Three of Patterson's comrades were shot out of hand soon after their capture, whilst others were threatened with the firing squad. After a harsh period of imprisonment, the survivors were released in late April on condition they did not return to Spain. All these men travelled home together, arriving in London on or around the 30th April. Patterson reached Penarth on 3rd May, and his newspaper account appeared a few days later. It was, perhaps, the only time in its history that the *Penarth Times* accepted Communist Party propaganda as gospel.

Wales was well represented in the International Brigade, and many a

> Welshman will return no more.... I was wounded and had to call it a day. But today more than half of our original battalion of 700-odd lie buried in Spain wrapped in their blanket - no pastor, no flowers, just the row of clenched fists, the salute of all anti-Fascist fighters.[65]

About a month before Bill Coles' and Harold Patterson's last fight, another Cardiffian had been seriously wounded in the battles around Madrid. Pat Murphy was born in Cardiff, in 1897, of first-generation Irish immigrant parents and saw active service in the First World War. An almost instinctive rebel - that stereotype of his national origins! - he was a seaman by calling, but so often in trouble with skippers that he spent more time ashore than at sea. An account given many years later recounted some of his story. In the autumn of 1936, he relates,

> I was the first volunteer from Cardiff.... I haunted Cardiff docks to get a passage on a ship trading to Spain, the main problem was to get a vessel that was destined to any port which the Republicans occupied. I did not relish the idea of being dumped amongst fascists in a Franco area. I confided to Len Jeffries about my aspirations, he told me that organisation was set up to help.[66]

Murphy was one of the earliest volunteers to reach Spain from the British Isles. Arriving at Albacete, where the International Brigades were based, in early December, 1936, he soon fell foul of the chief commissar, André Marty, by demanding that soldiers' councils be set up to arrive at decisions - including the election of officers - by discussion and vote. This was a practice prevalent in the anarchist militias, but it represented anathema to the Communist Party, which controlled the International Brigades. For this act of heresy, Murphy spent some time in the barracks' jailhouse. (If some accounts of Marty's methods are to be believed, Murphy was lucky to escape with his life.) Because of his military experience, he was released in order to join an advance 'task force' of the British Battalion, which was being sent to fight in Andalusia. Murphy saw action in the bitter campaign around Córdoba, in company with several brave Irishmen, with whom he soon forged close links. As soon as its job was done in the south, this '1st Company' was sent straight to the Madrid front to help with another emergency. Perhaps to Marty's disappointment, though many of his comrades fell, Pat Murphy survived these terrible encounters - though only just. During the fighting around Madrid, as an Irish comrade remembered

> We were lying in position on a ridge. Dinny Coady lay near me and another Irishman Pat Murphy, between us. A shell landed between Coady and Murphy. I immediately felt a sharp pain in my side. Murphy screamed. I glanced towards him. He was enveloped in a cloud of smoke and dust. But I could see his face ... he was ghastly pale. I got up and walked down to a ravine where our Company Headquarters section was posted, and told them to send up a stretcher at once. I thought Murphy had been badly hit. Then I got a Red Cross man to rip my clothes off. I had a deep wound under my armpit and a slight scratch on my leg.[67]

Murphy was rescued alive from the battlefield and spent the next two months (including the whole of the three-week battle of Jarama) recovering in hospital. Here he found time to write to the National Union of Seaman, asking for copies of the Union magazine *The Seaman* ('and other working class literature'[68]) to be sent out to the boys of the International Brigade, who were always sadly short of reading material and tobacco. Despite - or perhaps because of - a Catholic upbringing, Murphy deeply resented what he regarded as pro-Franco propaganda circulated by the Church. He undoubtedly derived ironic satisfaction from the fact that the Cardiff recruiting office for the International Brigades had been set up in the building situated exactly next door to the Catholic pro-Cathedral in Charles Street. At Albacete, he wrote

> the Cathedral was a splendid sight, more spectacular than the derelict shacks that God's children - the workers - existed in. The British R.C. press had previously printed reports of the gruesome antics of the popular Front with illustrations of skeletons propped against the outer walls of the edifice, supposed to have been drag'd from their tombs in the vaults. I spent ample time there to see if there was any signs of damage etc to substantiate this propaganda talk in the religiously fervent columns. Everything was in order throughout the building.[69]

By now, Murphy had come to regard himself as belonging to the Irish contingent rather than to the British, whose officers and ideas too closely resembled a kind of authority he wished not to fight for, but rather - if anything - against. Political attitudes amongst Irish comrades suited his maverick political personality, and he identified with them to the extent that several sources clearly (but mistakenly) regard him as Irish. Not long after his discharge from hospital, Murphy was again thrown into action, this time during the Republican offensive at Brunete (July 1937). His part in the attack on the township of Villanueva de la Canada was recorded by the leader of the Irish contingent, Frank Ryan, in the official History of the XV Brigade.

> The final storming of the town was a desperate affair, carried out just at nightfall ... The Americans and ourselves were trying to find cover in flat ground a few hundred yards away from the houses. Our aircraft and artillery had pounded the place well, but the church (which of course dominates every landscape here) kept standing. And from its tower, machine guns seriously hampered us. Just at dusk a crowd of women, children and old men, and about forty young men, came out the road, hands outstretched, calling 'Camaradas'. Pat Murphy and some others were behind a dung-pit. They thought the crowd were refugees. Pat got up and went to meet them, telling them, to drop their arms, if they had any. Just as he approached, a revolver barked, then grenades started to fly. For five minutes there was pandemonium, guns cracking, grenades bursting, and women and children shrieking. Pat, engaged in a hand-to-hand struggle, fell into a drain with his opponent, where he dispatched him. Beside him fell a little girl of about ten years who had been at the head of the group. 'Lie quiet, girlie', said Pat, and she smiled back as if she understood. A grenade burst in the drain and Pat was severely wounded in the groin.... It was all over; the last of the fascists had been accounted for. When the lads went around ... they found the little girl, two old women and three old men dead. It was at least a satisfaction that every single one of the fascists who had driven them in front of them as cover was also dead.[70]

Behind the lines, Murphy was patched up yet again, this time by the Welsh writer Alun Menai Williams, who was working as a medical orderly, and later gave evidence that 'Pat Murphy was very, very popular'[71]. This indomitable warrior remained true to his anarchist convictions, and always refused promotion. It is a matter for wonder, given his fearlessness in battle and the appalling casualty rate suffered generally by the Brigades, that Murphy survived the war. After Brunete, he was invalided home, and thereafter contented himself with sending encouraging letters, and even more encouraging cigarette supplies, to comrades still in Spain. He lived for many years afterwards in the Docks (where he is remembered by Joe Larreta as an *aficionado* of the 'North & South' in Louisa Street) and later in Grangetown. A few years before his death in 1974, he enjoyed helping Hywel Francis, during the researching of the latter's thesis about Wales and the Spanish War. In 1995, Pat Murphy's role in the Spanish Civil War was apparently immortalised in the Ken Loach-Jim Allen film *Land and Freedom*, which seems to draw on him for the character of 'Pat Coogan', and presents, in one of its dramatic action scenes, a version of the incident at Villanueva de la Cañada.

The Legionaire

When Pat Murphy was wounded for the first time, in January 1937, he was helping to defend the town of Las Rozas, object of a determined nationalist drive aiming to cut off the Corunna road and threaten the northern defences of Madrid from the rear. A few miles away, in the ranks of his advancing enemies, an infantryman in the 6th Battalion (*Bandera*) of the Foreign Legion, was Frank Thomas of Cyncoed. When the Spanish war broke out, Thomas was twenty-two years old and working in his father's business as a commercial traveller. In his unpublished account of his service in Spain, he states that, although a convinced anti-communist, his main reason for volunteering was a desire for adventure and glory, in contrast to the humdrum, ordinary life he was then leading. This yearning for experience and action - an escape from the mundane - was something instilled into that generation through countless novels and films. Almost regardless of class origins, and on both sides of the conflict, it was undoubtedly a widespread motivation for foreign volunteers to enlist in Spain. Yet this motive could often, and quite legitimately, co-exist in the same man with powerful ideals and political beliefs. In an interview published by the *Western Mail*, and sub-headed 'Fighting for his Principles', Frank Thomas' father stated:

> The last we heard from him he was in Burgos as a private in the Foreign Legion. He repeated his assertion that he was going to make a name for himself as great as any of his heroes. He has always believed the Communists are to blame for the world's ills and that they should be exterminated. Franco has given him a chance.[72]

The reporter added, in terms which remind us of the early pro-Franco leanings of this newspaper, 'I could see they were proud of him ... Frank Thomas is fighting for what he believes to be right'.

Never was a lightly-penned journalistic cliché more true. On the very day that Cardiffians were propping this paper, folded at the appropriate page, behind their boiled eggs, young Frank's *bandera*, was fighting its way, yard by yard and tree by tree, onto the heights of Carabanchel, overlooking Madrid. He joined this unit - part of the Francoist army of Africa, in the division commanded by Lieutenant-Colonel Asensio - before the end of October 1936, after reaching Burgos via a holiday cruise ship to Lisbon and undergoing rapid and rudimentary training. In the middle of November, Thomas took part in the last of a series of nationalist offensives against the heart of the

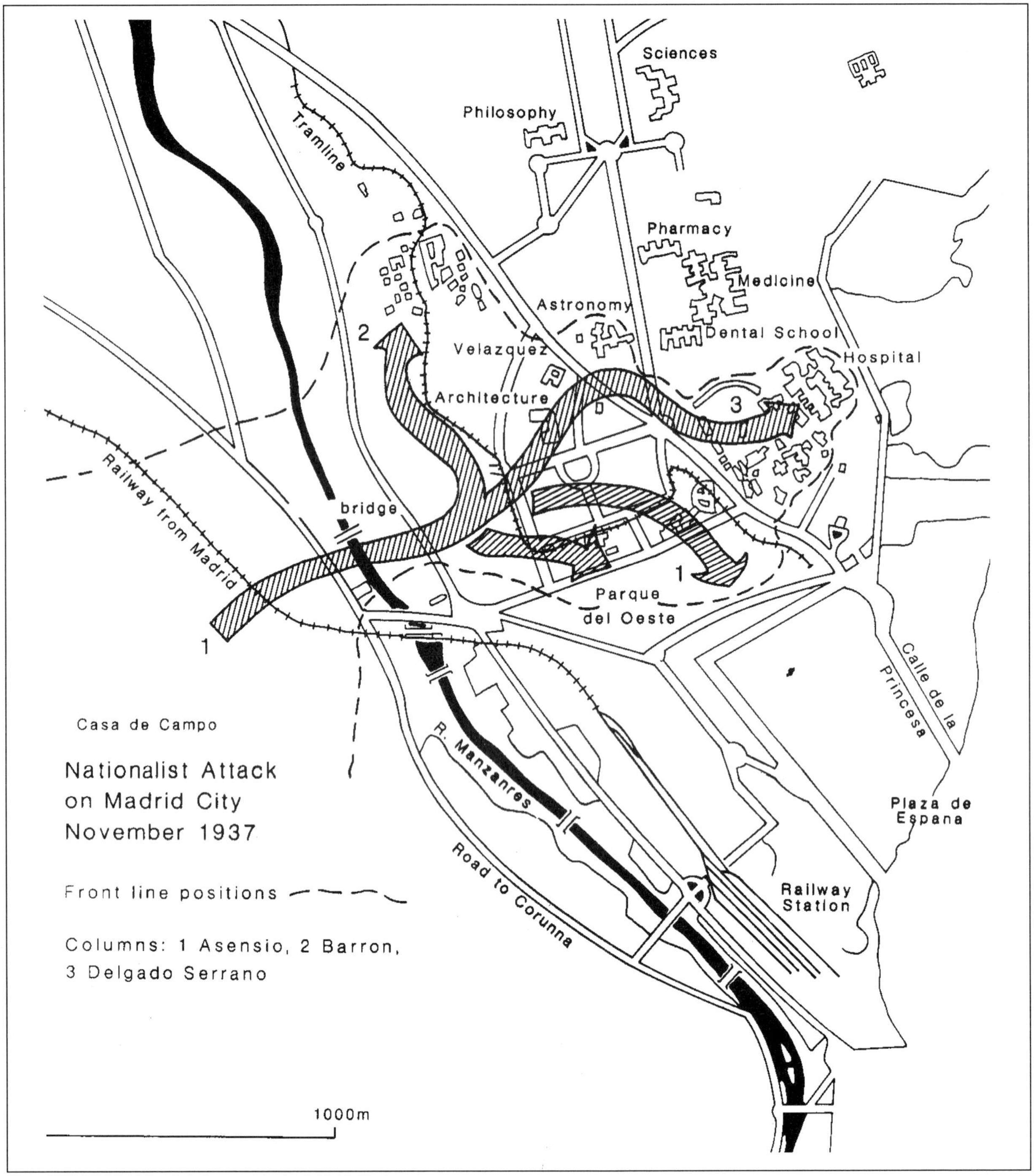

Map 4.
The Nationalist attack on Madrid City, November 1936.

capital city. Though, like its predecessors, the attack failed to capture Madrid, the fierce and bloody struggle in the University Park took Thomas to a position where he was looking down the heavily-barricaded main avenue (*Calle de la Princesa*) which led to the very centre of the capital. After distinguishing himself in action during the later advance against Las Rozas (see above), Thomas was - perhaps luckily for him - made batman to his company captain. As a result, he was not called upon to be part of the assault forces during the Jarama engagement (February 1937) which proved to be the most horrific pitched battle of the war. Yet, for this very reason, he was able to observe this awesome struggle more closely, and even with some mental detachment. On the day Bill Coles was killed, his fellow-Cardiffian must have been within less than a kilometre's proximity. In a remarkable unpublished memoir, written not long after the events it describes, Mr. Thomas pays grudging tribute to the resistance staged by the British Battalion against the fearsome Legionary units which were the elite troops of Franco's army.

> The enemy in front of us had been reinforced - at least this was the first time we had seen them - by the Fifteenth (English-speaking) Battalion and besides our being opposed by superior numbers, it must be candidly stated - with (after all) some national pride although I still consider their cause a false one - the latter presented us with more solid opposition than we were accustomed to ... One night in particular they made a bayonet charge against us at dusk ... momentarily the Bandera gave ground, only to recover and magnificently drive them back. I was fortunately on the spot to see it, but being armed only with the captain's lunch-basket, gave quite as much ground as any![73]

Thomas tells of the intense exchanges on the western and northern slopes of the Pingarrón ridge, where many of his and Pat Murphy's comrades met their deaths in close - at times hand-to-hand - combat. His own closest *compadre*, a 'White' (i.e. anticommunist) Russian, engaged in a battle where the skies above them were dominated by Soviet aircraft and pilots, was fatally wounded by British sniper fire.

The previous October, Frank Thomas had encountered a British press photographer who snapped some pictures and scribbled down a few personal details during a pause in the nationalist advance, at the town of Navalcarnero. The pictures were syndicated to newspapers in various parts of the world, appearing (among others) in the London *Daily Sketch* and the *Toronto Daily Star* as well as the *Western Mail*. It may have been a tiny taste of the fame that

**33.
Frank Thomas helping to man a captured enemy trench near Madrid, October 1936.**

the young Frank Thomas craved, but ironically he knew nothing about it. On his return to Navalcarnero for a well-deserved rest period some months later, Thomas noted that only 127 men survived of the 550 who had made up his *bandera* when it marched out towards Madrid. This rate of loss (some seventy seven per cent) exceeded even that sustained by the International Brigades, and is voluble testament to the ferocity of the fighting in which he had been almost continuously engaged for a period of three months.

Thomas himself only escaped the inferno - if by no means unscathed - through an amazing sequence of events. Following the brief respite referred to above, the Sixth *Bandera* was despatched southwards, in order to help stem a republican offensive against Toledo. During this campaign, Thomas - now promoted to corporal - found himself in occupation of a forward trench which was being enfiladed on both sides. His own squad of five men were killed or otherwise disabled around him. At length he himself was hit by a bullet which passed through the fleshy side of his face. His cheekbone was splintered though (as it proved) not shattered. However, as he tried to scramble back to the main lines, another bullet took him in the leg. He had to roll uphill through barbed wire in order to gain safety. This excruciating but at least short journey was followed by an agonisingly long one down back through the *Montes de Toledo* to the field hospital, slung like a sack across the back of a mule.

In this battle, Thomas' unit had been pitched against the best troops in the republican army - Enrique Lister's Eleventh Division. Lister himself later boasted (in his memoirs) that his men 'destroyed two battalions of moors, and three legionary *banderas*, among other units'[74]. Though this was an exaggeration, it seems that Thomas was lucky to leave the front when he did. At any rate, a few weeks later, he was sent to convalesce in hospital in the beautiful medieval town of Cáceres, located in Extremadura (western Spain) not far from the Portuguese border. As it happened, this town was the headquarters of another battalion of the Foreign Legion - the unique Fifteenth *Bandera*, composed of Irishmen who had volunteered to fight in Spain. Its members were mostly citizens of what was then the Irish Free State. The majority had been motivated to enlist on religious grounds, outraged as they were by the widespread atrocities against the Catholic clergy committed by 'the red forces' during the early months of the war. Thomas himself bears witness to this phenomenon.

> We found [at Carabanchel] the half-burned body of the parish priest, his little church turned into a communist hall and the cross above the door replaced by the hammer and sickle done in red paint, and the doors and walls defaced by slogans, lewdness and the initials of various political parties.[75]

Thomas quickly became friendly with Irish volunteers who were being treated in the hospital. He learned that the Irish Brigade had recently been withdrawn from the line and was preparing to return home. He managed to get an introduction to their commander, General O'Duffy, who promised to help him. In mid-June, he was smuggled out of Spain in the company of his new friends and spirited aboard an Ireland-bound ferry ship at Lisbon. Thomas reached Cardiff and home, via Dublin, a fortnight later.

Technically, Frank Thomas had deserted; and, as we shall see, he was by no means the only volunteer, on both sides, to do so. As a man who regarded himself as a professional soldier, he was acutely conscious of the meaning of his action, and he did not arrive at his decision lightly. He had received scant recognition for a battlefield dedication amounting to heroism, and had become convinced of a serious decline in standards of fighting efficiency and discipline in the Legion - a factor contributing to the closeness of his own encounter with death. But in addition political feelings coexisted with the personal. Although the fact did nothing to change his opinion about the enemy's cause, he had become less enamoured of the nationalist side. In particular he felt

**34.
Frank Thomas today, with his nationalist army cap (or gorillo).**

resentful of an increasingly anti-British element in their attitudes and propaganda. (This was undoubtedly a reaction to the more pronounced pro-republican inclination of British opinion in the wake of Guernica.) On the eve of his last battle, he looked out on the undulating landscape of the *montes de Toledo* serene under the stars:

> I think it was at that moment that I first realised the age-old idiocy which is war; something radiating from those beautiful peaks conveying more to me than all the wrecked homes and lives I had seen; something of the horror of fratricide which civil war wreaks.... and yet something of that nationalism for which both sides are fighting - the one for age-old traditions, faith an equitable utopia.... Whatever the final outcome of this present war the mighty clash of these two opposing cultures will bear a great part in the ultimate moulding of the future Spain.[76]

At twenty-three, Frank Thomas was a hard-bitten veteran. Yet the feelings he expresses here were shared with many of the participants on both (or all) sides in the war, from the famous, like George Orwell, to many less well known. Fundamentally, it was one of disillusion. They learned that war, if sometimes necessary, is ultimately neither romantic nor glorious; and that it invariably and inevitably compromises the cause for which it is fought.

The Internationals - Part Two

Across the wide valleys of the Jarama and the Tagus, amongst the opposed ranks of the International Brigades, similar doubts to those of Frank Thomas were stirring in hearts and minds. But no more here than among the nationalists could these misgivings be permitted actual utterance. This had far wider resonances than the usual need for morale among the armies themselves. On both sides the propaganda war was seen as a desperately serious element of the conflict. Rigid political loyalty was required and imposed among civilians and military alike. For its part, the Communist Party was engaged in an international campaign to record and disseminate profuse statements of uncompromising commitment. William Rust, the chief *Daily Worker* correspondent in Spain (and himself one-time commander of the British Battalion) collected such statements in order to encourage those on the home front to support - or even to join - the struggle.

Gilbert Taylor was the manager of Collett's, the communist bookshop in the Castle Arcade which has already been mentioned as a centre of pro-republican activity in Cardiff. We can easily imagine that on occasions, urging a customer to have the courage of his left-wing convictions, Taylor may have elicited the natural response of: 'well, if you're such a good comrade, why don't you go to Spain yourself?'. Some on the 'admin. side' of the recruitment process were impervious to such a goad. Taylor was not and accordingly, went. Interviewed by Rust not long before his death in action at Calaceite (Aragon) in the spring of 1938, and conscious of the importance of propaganda, he provided perfect copy:

> I may say that I loathe everything in any way connected with being a soldier. I hate both the fact and the necessity of having to drill and salute and wear uniform and shoot. But I believe quite honestly that the aid which I shall be asked to give within the next few months will end fascism in Spain, and in so doing will help to save England the necessity of making the experiment itself.[77]

An equally committed Cardiff comrade was seaman Bill Morrisey, who immersed himself so thoroughly in the cause that he became a stereotype. Morrisey's letters from Spain illustrate a fairly common phenomenon of those days of struggle - the deliberate effacement of the self in favour of the abstract collective will of the Party. He wrote a series of letters to a Newport comrade, for no personal reason, but simply in order to help this particular section of

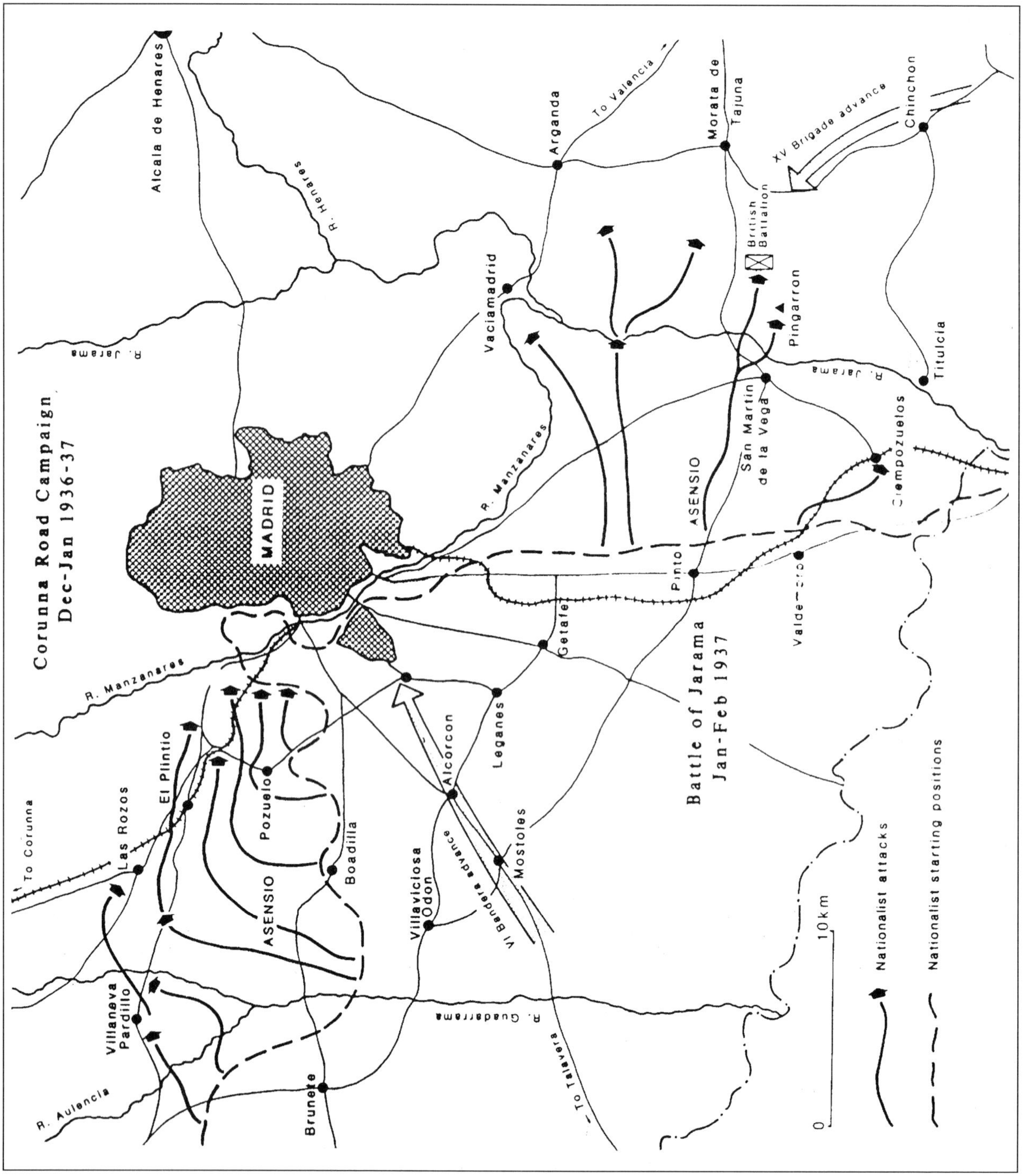

Map 5.
The battles for Madrid in the winter of 1936-37.

the 'home front' to raise consciousness about and support for the International Brigades. Full of rousing slogans and party platitudes, the letters reveal next to nothing about the writer himself or his experiences. Indeed, reading them, it comes across as almost embarrassingly personal when, at one point, he scribbles the hasty afterthought: 'I forgot to mention I am from Cardiff'.[78]

Morrisey seems to have been mainly based in the office at Albacete, headquarters of the International Brigades, where one of his duties was to act as 'official' letter-writer - a sort of political pen-pal. After returning home, he remained (as it were) mobilised in the cause. In February 1939, he spoke at the pro-Republican meeting held in Penarth, already described. It may be guessed that the characterless prose of the *Penarth Times* reporter fails to convey the passionate character of Morrisey's contribution.

> He recalled the manner in which precautions were taken to catch and kill a savage leopard which had broken loose in this country. No efforts, however, seem to have been made to account for three savage beasts which were loose in Europe. He referred to Franco, Hitler and Mussolini.[79]

Another speaker on this Penarth occasion was a locally-born man, Robert Peters, who had emigrated to Canada some years before (aged only 16) in search of work. He worked for a shipping company on the Great Lakes, and became politically aware through a local struggle for union recognition. When the Spanish War broke out, he volunteered to join the Canadian Mackenzie-Papineau unit. In the event, there were not enough Canadians to form a battalion, and Peters was transferred to the British. Like Pat Murphy, he was wounded in the early stages of the Brunete offensive (July, 1937). He takes up the story in his own words:

> We went up to Sierra de Guadarrama for the Battle of Brunete. Casualties were heavy, and the heat and dust were unbearable ... I got a bullet in my back: it lodged against my spine. Eventually I was considered fit enough to return to my unit, the bullet still inside me, and served as a dispatch rider. Through the bouncing about, the bullet travelled up my shoulder and down my right arm. It was successfully removed in an operation. If I ever did anything useful in my life, this was the one thing I have done ... we volunteered, we went there for a purpose ... Back home I made some speeches to try and get milk for children in Spain. My mother was very proud of me.[80]

Peters - who now lives in retirement in Bexley (Kent) - has several distinctions. For one thing, he seems to be the only surviving veteran of the International Brigades from all those connected with Cardiff and district. For another, he served one of the longest continuous tours of duty of any volunteer from Wales (and possibly from Britain as a whole) being enlisted for twenty-two months, and only finally shaking the dust of Spain from his feet a few weeks before the capture of Catalonia by Franco.

**35.
Robert Peters during his sojourn in Canada.**

Despite taking place at the same time and in (roughly) the same place as that of battle-scarred warriors like Murphy, Thomas and Peters, the experience of Harry Stratton was markedly different. Stratton - whom we have already encountered taking a petition by taxi to Stanley Baldwin - joined the Cardiff branch of the Communist Party in 1936. A native of Swansea, he had only recently come to live in Cardiff (home of his wife, Winnie's, family) and moved into a new house in Ely. Being self-employed and from a middle-class business background, he was a rather untypical militant. But when he heard that an old Swansea mate, to whom he felt close, had volunteered for the Internationals, Stratton straightaway decided to go to Spain. He didn't discuss the matter with his wife, who was not of his political persuasion; but party officials assured him that she and their two children would be suitably looked after. Not long afterwards, having been taken across France via the communist-organised 'underground railway', he crossed into Spain from Perpignan, and was quartered for a time in the main reception camp in Figueras fort. Arriving at Albacete on 6th February 1937, his group were given a pep-talk in the town's bullring by Commissar Peter Kerrigan, and then went off to for military training at Madrigueras, a nearby village which formed the British billets. Only the next day, they heard that their Battalion was to leave for the front. Bill Coles and the rest of the 600 who had completed training left for what was soon to become the valley of death - Jarama. Such was the carnage of the battle and the need for men to plug yawning gaps in the line, that Stratton himself was drafted to the front only a week later, having never even held - leave alone fired - a rifle! On 27th February, the last day of the three-week battle, he was in a reserve unit, preparing for a counter-attack on the main enemy strongpoint of Pingarrón hill. It was an operation as meaningless and suicidal as any offensive on the western front during the war of 1914-18. In the first assaults, the Lincoln (U.S.) Battalion came close to being annihilated. Stratton's platoon was preparing to 'go over the top' as part of a second wave, when the operation was mercifully called off.

36.
Top: Canadian comrades, including Robert Peters (on the left) on the way to Spain in early 1937.

37.
Bottom: Robert Peters today.

38.
A group of comrades, including Harry Stratton (in front) and Bill Morrisey (immediately behind him) taken in Albacete, autumn 1937.

Stratton subsequently endured a long and miserable period of trench warfare. He had some ability in making sketches of what he saw around him, and this, along with a keen sense of humour, made life bearable. Despite these attributes, he managed to get into trouble with officers and party authorities for supporting complaints about the quality and regularity of food supplies at the front. As a result he was evidently classified as unreliable, and relegated to duties behind the lines. During the battle of Brunete, which dominated republican strategy in the summer of 1937, he served in various medical units based in the vicinity of the Escorial palace, to the north-west of Madrid. Later, hearing that his wife and family were in some distress, Stratton applied to Commissar Will Paynter for repatriation on compassionate grounds. In August, he got back to Albacete hoping for his demobilisation papers, but instead found himself interrogated and despatched to the notorious 'political re-education centre' known as Camp Lucas. Not surprisingly, in the rigorously 'corrective' regime of the camp, he contracted a serious illness. When he eventually recovered, he was at last able to secure his repatriation. Shortly before Stratton left Albacete for good, he posed for a souvenir shot with Bill Morrisey and some other Welsh pals in the studio of a local photographer. At last, with the blessing of the Party, Stratton came safely back to Cardiff (via Barcelona) in the autumn of 1937. Like Morrisey, he continued to be a loyal party worker for many years thereafter.

The least conventionally heroic - if, undeniably, tragic - of all the stories of Cardiff's connections with the Spanish Civil War is that associated with T.A.R. Hyndman. Tony Hyndman (or Tom, as some knew him in later life) was born in a Tiger Bay pub around 1910. When he was still a child his parents moved, to take over another pub (probably 'The Neville') in Grangetown. Like his exact contemporary, Bill Coles, he grew up a strong lad, with, to quote Windsor Davies, a 'fine pair of shoulders'. Lacking any alternative prospect, Hyndman signed up with the Coldstream Guards. After discharge, he drifted to London and joined the crowd of faceless, hopeless unemployed. One spring day in 1933, loitering in Piccadilly Circus, Hyndman was approached by (or perhaps himself approached) a tall, upper-class man of about his own age. There was an immediate physical attraction between the two men.

39.
T.A.R. Hyndman pictured (probably) on holiday with Spender in 1933.

The stranger was Stephen Spender, unknown at that particular juncture, but on the point of becoming one of the best-known young English poets. Hyndman became Spender's 'secretary' - a euphemism for live-in lover, plus, in effect, house-person. In the next few years, they went on frequent holidays together to what were then obscure and inexpensive Mediterranean resorts. Through Spender, Hyndman became an associate member of what is generally regarded as the most significant circle of British writers of the present century, authors whose names sound like a roll-call of today's 'English Literature' syllabus; W.H. Auden, Christopher Isherwood - both homosexuals - and Spender himself. On one occasion in 1935, Hyndman spent a holiday in Amsterdam with all three of these, plus the celebrated novelist E.M. Forster, along with the other three male partners concerned. In 1934, he shared with Auden (generally regarded as the greatest English poet of this century) the dedication of Spender's book of short stories *The Burning Cactus.*

As this illustrates, the relationship between Hyndman and Spender quickly grew into one of genuine emotional depth. Their life together was fraught with difficulties - not only the nagging insecurity of gay domesticity at a time when homosexuality was a criminal offence, but problems arising from the fact that Hyndman, though not unintelligent, was totally untutored in 'literature' and completely bewildered by the intellectually high-powered and socially exclusive circle into which fate had thrust him. The inescapable social and economic gulf between the two lovers was intensified by the unbridgeable abyss of their different mental cultures. Undoubtedly, for Spender, Hyndman's social origins were part of the attraction. In the 1930s, left-wing intellectuals, in what now seems a pathetic fallacy, attempted to atone for centuries of oppression (real and imagined) and to abolish their socially-patronising habits. Removing themselves from this pedestal, they placed the 'working class' there instead, in the obsessive but hopeless attempt to identify with - and even to share - the experiences of the struggling masses.

Throughout his autobiography, Spender referred to Tony Hyndman as 'Jimmy Younger'; and he writes

> I was in love, as it were, with his background, his soldiering, his working-class home. Nothing moved me more than to hear him tell stories of the Cardiff streets of Tiger Bay, of his uncle who was in the Salvation Army and who asked for his trumpet to be buried beside him in his grave, so that when he awoke on the day of judgement he might blow a great blast of hallelujah on it. When Jimmy talked of such things ... I was very close to certain emotions awakened in childhood by the workers, who to us seemed at the same time coarse, unclean, and yet with something about them of forbidden fruit, and also of warm-heartedness which suddenly flashed across the cold gulf of class, secret and unspoken.[81]

Some readers might be tempted to respond to such writing with one or more suitably dismissive monosyllables. Indeed, it succeeds only in betraying a kind of inverted snobbery. It was a feeling produced by the fashionable culture of modernism - an anti-romantic desire to efface the selfishness and guilt produced by inherited property and privilege. For thousands of sons and daughters of the ruling class, this pitiable and hopeless yearning led them towards communism, or into fascism, or both; indeed, in this context, it makes little difference.

But the problems of the Spender-Hyndman relationship were compounded by the fact that, unlike Tony's, Stephen's sexuality was ambivalent. In the autumn of 1936, the poet began to involve himself in the aid-Spain movement. Soon he met a Spanish girl domiciled in London, and within a few weeks they were married. Hyndman was obliged to move out of Spender's flat and make himself scarce. In a mood of bitter jealousy and resentment, he was easy prey for the recruiting predator. Esmond Romilly - nephew of Winston Churchill - had just returned from Spain a hero, having covered himself with glory defending the oppressed masses of Madrid. Hyndman had already joined the Communist Party - on the rebound, as it were, from Spender - and in the

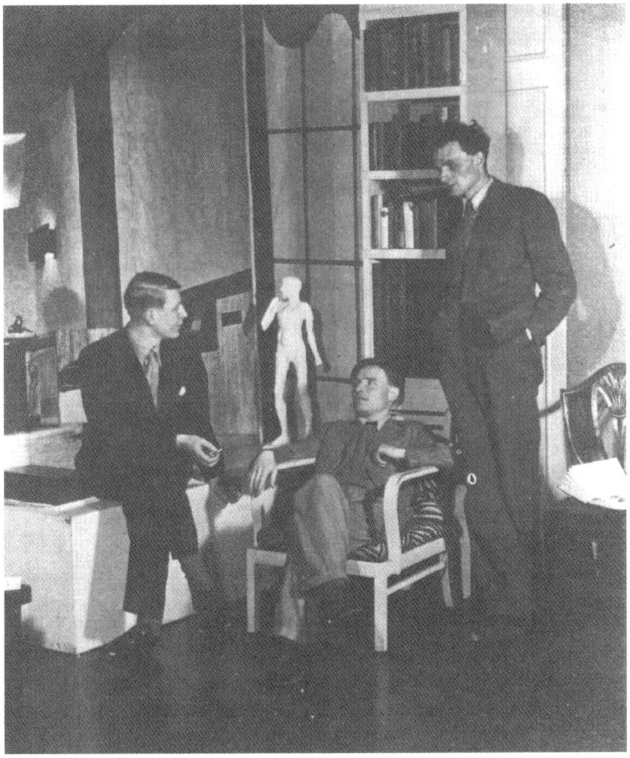

43.
Stephen Spender (standing), with W.H. Auden and Chistopher Isherwood, around the time his relationship with Hyndman began.

course of his political work had become friendly with Romilly's brother, Giles. Now, both he and Giles were inspired by Esmond's example to volunteer for the International Brigades. Hyndman later gave an account of how Giles invited him home to Mayfair for tea:

> Mrs Romilly had an engaging sense of drama, of theatre. 'Two sons', she said. 'Both in the same war. I must speak to the Colonel'. She reached for the telephone. 'My father', said Giles. 'He lives in the country, for health reasons. Have some more walnut cake'. His mother was now listening to her husband. 'Yes, my dear. Of course. You are quite right. I will tell Giles and his friend. He was in the Guards you know. No: I don't think he was an officer...' Mrs Romilly turned to us. 'The Colonel has given me a message ... you must both go to the Army and Navy [Stores], get yourselves well kitted out with the best boots they have, besides a good supply of their warmest underwear. All on his account ... He is an old soldier. You have his blessing. Now wait a moment'. She went upstairs and came down with the longest scarf I have ever seen. She gave it to me. 'I knitted this myself, for my husband during the war. It is to be worn next to your skin, around your stomach, to keep you warm'. She gave me a kiss. 'Now, some sherry'.[82]

After taking part in this farcical scene - as if from a novel by Evelyn Waugh - the two young men set off for Spain via Brussels, where Christopher Isherwood vainly attempted to dissuade them from their reckless plan. Within a few weeks they were in action at Jarama. Nothing in Hyndman's training or experience as a soldier had prepared him for this kind of battle. In various later interviews and writings, Hyndman recorded several different - in some respects, contradictory - versions of what happened to him in Spain. Matters are further complicated by the fact that Spender, too, could never bring himself to publish the full, unexpurgated story, and his memoirs are especially unreliable over the Spanish episodes of their relationship. In one account, (included in Spender's autobiography) Hyndman related how his troubles began even before the battle. There were, he recalled

> outbreaks of unrest in the village [of Madrigueras] among the troops, the Scotsmen being the worst offenders, and [they opened a] prison, a real one with armed guards, and cells which were none too savoury. On account of refusing to obey an order with which I didn't agree, I was put in it for a while.... Profound disillusionment.... I fell out with the Communist Party here and in my relationship with them a rot set in which affected much of what happened later.[83]

During the battle of Jarama (Hyndman told Cardiff solicitor Mr. Chris Short many years later) he was cut off, and hid from advancing enemy troops behind the dead body of a young Glaswegian. He managed to escape from Frank Thomas' comrades but not from his own: he was located, put in jail once more and threatened with execution as a deserter. In another version, which he published in 1976, Hyndman appears rather more battle-worthy, helping to save machine-guns which had been stuck under an overturned lorry, and successfully installing them in the front line, despite being strafed by Italian planes. In the trenches, between furious republican counter-attacks, Hyndman:

> could hear the wounded moaning and calling to us as they lay between the lines. At the end of a week I knew the meaning of war. I can still see the blood and the dead faces; worse still the expression in the eyes of the dying. I felt no anti-Fascist anger, but only overwhelming pity.[84]

Reading between all the available lines, the truth seems to be that such was the shock, horror and confusion of the first moments of battle that both Hyndman and Romilly - trained guardsman and naive student - simply ran away. (Quite understandably, so did dozens of others.) At some point before the end of the great Jarama battle, their mutual friend, T.C. Worsley, made a brief visit to the front, on a mission perhaps partly inspired by Spender. By dint of sheer persistence, Worsley managed to locate his friends at dead of night, on a dark hillside, enlivened by stray bullets and lit up by sporadic shellfire. They explained what had happened.

> Tony had been in the front line up at the top of the hill. The Brigade had been rushed up in lorries to help hold the attack: there were no trenches or prepared positions, just the ridge thickly dotted with olive trees.... Tony described how you could hear the Moors howling, and how they came near enough actually to be seen before our men, without any machine guns, were driven back. This was the Brigade's first taste of action and it is not surprising that the retreat became a run ... (Some of the men of the company got so out of touch that they did not link up with the company for two days.)[85]

Following a short period at the front in non-combatant duties, Hyndman was returned to Albacete and imprisoned. Meanwhile, Spender, full of remorse and anxiety over Hyndman, had found an excuse to go to Spain. He was interviewed by Harry Pollitt, joined the Party, and undertook a reporting commission about the Spanish War for the *Daily Worker*, desperately hoping to locate his lover at some point of the journey. Later, back in London, he heard that Hyndman was in trouble with the Brigade and the Party, and that he was suffering from a stomach ulcer. Again Spender travelled to Spain, this time as a delegate attending a Communist writers' conference in Madrid. He got to Albacete and was brusquely informed by the commissars that it would be bad propaganda were 'Jimmy' to return to Britain. After a great effort of persuasion by Spender, Hyndman agreed to stay, as long as he could be employed usefully and safely behind the lines. But no sooner had Spender left than Hyndman deserted, in company with another disillusioned comrade, John Lepper. They got as far as Valencia, where they were picked up by republican police. Caught this time in a flagrant case of desertion, the firing-squad was now a distinct possibility. Hyndman and Lepper were sent to Camp Lucas to await trial.

According to his own account, Spender's 'life was dominated by my concern for Jimmy ... I was simply determined to do everything in my power to prevent him dying in Spain'[86]. To this end, Spender even managed to gain an audience in Valencia with the republican foreign minister, Julio Alvarez del Vayo. He returned to Albacete, and was taken to see the members of the tribunal

**41.
T.A.R. Hyndman in 1976.**

appointed to hear the case, who assured him that the miscreant's life would be spared - but that he would have to serve out his sentence in the prison camp. On his subsequent visits to Spain, Pollitt regularly checked on Hyndman's condition. As Hyndman recalled in a sentence heavy with socio-sexual ironies: 'In Harry Pollitt's opinion, I was told later, I was an ordinary, decent, working class chap who had got into the hands of the kind of intellectuals the party could well do without'.[87]

After three very unpleasant months, Hyndman gained his liberty and returned to London in September 1937. His relationship with Spender was not yet over, but following the latter's successful second marriage (in the late 1940s) it gradually petered out. After a life of many vicissitudes, working in left-wing publishing circles and then in theatre administration, Hyndman came back to his native city for good in 1970. For some time he worked as a porter at the Queen's Hotel in St. Mary Street and, grateful for help with his drink problem, gave a hand in his spare time at the St. Dyfrig's care unit on Fitzhamon Embankment. He ended his days, Chris Short recalls, 'in a rather squalid flat in Taff Embankment, Grangetown.'[88]

When he was released from his Spanish jail, a further condition had been imposed on Hyndman by the Party: that he should never speak or write about his experiences in Spain. He broke this parole in very short order. In 1939, Spender and John Lehmann co-edited a poetry collection called *Poems for Spain*. There was nothing routine or ordinary about this publication - it became, arguably, the most celebrated anthology of English verse published in the twentieth century. For propaganda reasons, the editors deliberately sought to include work by writers who were not from the traditional social and educational background of English poets. Thus, as a result of the Spanish Civil War, a Cardiff man who was on intimate terms with the Cambridge intellectual mandarins, an uneducated Grangetown boy who became familiar with the renowned *literati* of Bloomsbury, found a niche in literary history.

Poems for Spain

Hyndman's poem describes a situation which was happening also in the enemy's lines, among the trenches manned by Frank Thomas. His words express the same disillusionment (in Spanish, *desengaño*) as that arrived at by his fellow-Cardiffian, a spirit of experience in which enemies can sometimes unite. The poem is called 'Jarama Front'.

I tried not to see,
But heard his voice.
How brown the earth
And green the trees.
One tree was his.
He could not move.
Wounded all over,
He lay there, moaning.

I hardly knew;
I tore his coat.
It was easy -
Shrapnel had helped.

But he was dying
And the blanket sagged.
'God bless you, Comrades,
He will thank you'.
That was all.
No slogan,
No clenched fist
Except in pain.[89]

Poems for Spain had an immediate and lasting influence on writing and on political attitudes in the English-speaking world, in Cardiff as much as New York. Whilst Bill Coles and Gilbert Taylor lost their lives, and whilst Tony Hyndman and Frank Thomas were losing their illusions, back in Windermere Avenue, near Roath Park Lake, a teenage boy was inspired by dreams of glorious martydom in Spain in the cause of freedom. Dannie Abse was a romantically impressionable fourteen-year-old when the Spanish War began and the event proved to be the epiphany of his life, the crucible in which his personality was created. Like thousands of other idealistic young people, he was captivated by *Poems for Spain*, which came out just at the time that the Republic's resistance finally crumbled. Like many others, he became determined that despite the verdict of the guns, its cause would never be

**42.
Dannie Abse with his mother, around 1939.**

extinguished. Arguably, nowadays, Cardiff's most celebrated literary figure, Abse was born into a well-known and populous tribe of Welsh Jews, which partook intimately of the middle- and working-class life of Cardiff (and South-East Wales generally). It was a time of deeply-rooted, and often public, anti-semitism in many parts of Britain, and rampant persecution of Jews in Germany. Dannie's domestic world was dominated by his two elder brothers, Wilfred and Leo, both of them intelligent and opinionated young men, who disagreed volubly on many things - but not on the question of support for the Spanish Republic. There were impassioned speeches at the dinner table; impromptu debates in the sitting room; passions stirred up by the reading of the *Left Review*. Above all, there was the heroic story of John Cornford, communist poet, warrior and martyr, killed in Spain on his twenty-first birthday. No wonder that young Dannie's adolescent mind was blown by Spain.

What intensified this situation was Leo's close friendship with Sid Hamm, a Pontypridd-born student at Cardiff Technical College, with whom he helped to found the Cardiff United Youth Movement. Together they would go to the Sunday hustings in Llandaff Fields - where Dannie

> first became excited by the power of words ... listening to my brother Leo - who would one day become an MP - gesticulating on a soap box ... and painting with words the bloody pictures of the war in Spain....[90]

43.
Sid Hamm, as he appeared on the leaflet distributed at the Cardiff memorial meeeting, later recalled by Dannie Abse.

Sid Hamm sometimes visited the Abse home to feast on their mother's sardines-on-toast. He, too, was a role-model for Dannie. Hamm was a popular figure in student and left-wing politics, a keen sportsman, and secretary of the Students' Union. He had joined the Communist Party in Cardiff, and in April 1937, was one of a party of twenty-seven Welsh volunteers for the International Brigades who left Cardiff for Spain. Three months later, he was killed during the battle of Brunete. The letter which is reproduced here [Appendix 2] was written about two weeks before his death somewhere on the arid plains west of Madrid. It gives a memorable impression of the character of this nineteen-year-old idealist.

In his semi-autobiographical novel *Ash On a Young Man's Sleeve*, Dannie Abse describes attending a memorial meeting for Sid Hamm (called 'Jimmy Ford' in the book) to hear Leo speak from the platform in condemnation of the policy of non-intervention.

> We sat there in the bare October Hall in the days of blackshirts, Potato Jones, Unemployment and Tommy Farr. Mrs Mary Ford walked in just as the speaker was thumping the table, making the water shake in the glass as he shouted, 'THERE CAN BE NO VICTORY WITHOUT SACRIFICE' ... all the audience eyed her pinched, translucent face, her frail shoulders draped in black. Mr. Thomas who

> had come to sit behind me said, 'He was just a kid'. And then, 'It's a hell of a world' ... The communist, Alan Fellows, spoke to a group of sympathisers gathered around Mary Ford and her mother-in-law ... Distinctly I heard Jimmy Ford's mother saying, 'It's all very well, Mr. Fellows, but you're not dead in Spain ... The portly chairman interceded: 'That's not fair, Mrs. Ford, Alan is doing a fine job....' If I was bigger (Dannie thought to himself) perhaps I could go to Spain. It was worth fighting for. Maybe if I got killed they'd have a memorial meeting for me.... 'If you feel so strongly about Spain,' I said (to Leo), 'why don't you go there?' Leo gazed down at me from his 21-year old eyes, as if he had been struck a blow.[91]

In writing his novel in the 1950s, Abse drew on background images of the Spanish war by other writers, like Miguel Hernandez and Ernest Hemingway, to reconstruct the last hours of 'Jimmy Ford'. We know so little about Hamm - 'the personification of youth'[92], as his memorial pamphlet put it - that it seems appropriate to reproduce this passage:

> At Brunete the International Brigade had marched through the dark; nobody dared to speak at all, but the night air hummed with the murmur of marching thousands.... Before dawn trickled its grey oil into the Spanish skies the various units had taken up their positions. In the dawn light Jimmy Ford looked at his silhouetted comrades for comfort. The man on his right was from Manchester - that's all he knew about him. Yesterday each had mingled through the lines looking for someone from his home town. And when they found a compatriot from a town away, or a street away, they would talk avidly, their location of birth giving them some kinship. Names of streets, pubs, dance halls were swopped as if they were names of exotic treasures. To be born in Cardiff and to meet a man from Newport was not to be solitary....[93]

In the mid-1930s, Dannie Abse was a pupil (of all places) at the Catholic high school, St. Illtyd's College, in Splott. The school was run by the De la Salle Brothers, a teaching order of clerics in minor vows, founded in the seventeenth century by a French philanthropist, but whose modern Cardiff mission was largely staffed by expatriates from the Irish Free State. The boys they taught were mainly drawn from Catholic families of the lower middle class, which today would be called 'upwardly mobile'. In his teenage years, Abse was a keen sportsman, an eager pupil, and equally indifferent to the spiritual claims of Judaism and Catholicism. Until 1937, nothing in his locally eccentric cultural background had affected his happy integration into the life of St. Illtyd's. The Spanish Civil War changed this: suddenly, Abse found himself in a minority of one, the only boy in the school who supported the Republic, and surrounded by teachers and schoolfriends who were more-or-less committed supporters of Franco.

> 'Do you know what the Reds would do if they came here?' said one of the brothers in his black grieving gown. 'Why boy, they'd burn me down and the school wid me', and when my fist clenched I think he mistakenly assumed I was giving a surreptitious communist salute.[94]

At least metaphorically clenching one fist in the Popular Front salute, this attitude soon meant that Dannie had to clench both of them in earnest in order to resist a challenge from a fellow-member of the school rugby team. The two youngsters had a bruising scrap in a lane behind Splott Road, because Dannie's adversary 'saw Franco as a knight on a white horse, a protector of nuns'[94]. Another St. Illtyd's boy displayed a very similar spirit of chivalry which he expressed in the alternative way. The only item to appear in the school magazine during the period of the Spanish war which made any reference to the conflict was a poem - but not by the hand of Dannie Abse. Instead, it was the work of a boy one year older, Mostyn Gibbs, who called it 'La Cruz de España' ('The Cross of Spain'):

If old Don Quixote came again
To canter down through tortured Spain,
His tranced mind would surely clear
And worthy foes should know his spear.

If Roland came to proud Castille,
His mighty horn would shattering peal,
Rousing his warriors to ride
In service of the Crucified.

Stout Cortez, the Conquistador,
Would sail for Spain with legions more
In galleons whose banners told
Of loyal steel in place of gold.

O, all the Saints of God who taught,
And all the men of arms who fought,

And all the admirals of the Main,
Would rally to the Cross of Spain.[95]

Despite their teenage pretension, these lines of Mostyn Gibbs express a feeling about Spain no less deeply-felt, nor less valid, than that which Dannie Abse - 'moved almost to tears ... by those who sang or cried as they defended themselves against Franco's guns'[96] - experienced when he made his first attempts at verse in 1939. Though none of his own juvenile apprentice-work survives, Abse looks back on his romantic-revolutionary feelings about poetry and politics in a recent poem called 'Sixth Form Poet':

When my acne almost cleared
I fell in love with humankind.
I wanted to requisition Poetry.
A revolution in my mind.

To the barricades not the court,
my gorgeous rage would console.
Though love be blind it sees
with the optic nerve of the soul.

Poetry is written in the brain
but the brain is bathed in blood.
I sang no praises for the King,
I, laureate to Robin Hood.[96]

Neither of these two sensitive Cardiff adolescents, Catholic conservative nor Jewish socialist, was old enough, even by the time the Spanish War ended in 1939, seriously to contemplate taking up arms for the causes they espoused so fervently in their intellects and in their emotions. However, in the Second World War, Mostyn Gibbs fought in the desert with the Eighth Army and then through much of the equally terrible Italian campaign of 1944-5. Later in life, he travelled in Spain extensively for business purposes and, on one occasion (in the 1950s), visited some of the battle sites of the Civil War. But it seems he never developed his youthful literary aspirations. In 1940, Dannie Abse went to London, where he completed his training as a doctor - a learning-process which included coping nightly with the wounded in the midst of the horror of the Blitz. Meanwhile, he pursued the vocation which was to make him one of the foremost Welsh writers of his generation.

The loss of idealism may lead to scepticism, even to cynicism, but it can also open the door to understanding. The spirit which (hopefully) prevails is not that nothing matters enough for permanent bitterness, but simply that trust and co-operation matter more. It was this spirit of reconciliation which moved some observers of the Spanish War even at the time. In the autumn of 1995, the National Museum of Wales Gallery acquired a painting by Edward Burra, dating from 1936, entitled 'Red Cloaked Figure'. Burra (1905-76) returned from one of his frequent trips to Spain only days before the outbreak of the Civil War. In Madrid he had witnessed scenes of violence, including the burning of a church, which sickened him. 'It was terrifying: constant strikes, churches on fire, and pent-up hatred everywhere. Everybody knew that something appalling was about to happen'[97]. Burra painted a bloody picture of the war, but one which has the ambiguity of poetry. Two mysterious visitors are watching a scene of carnage in a Spanish street. The right-hand foreground is dominated by a convent wall with characteristic barred windows - one of which appears to have been forced open, suggesting violation of the building (and, perhaps, its occupants). All along this wall, and at the feet of the observing couple, lie murdered bodies - very suggestive of the lines of Spanish dead set out for identification, as pictured by contemporary newsreels. In the background, two nuns seem to be ministering to the victims, but beyond them, in the mid-distance of a deep perspective, other groups are seen to be still engaged in acts of murder.

44.
Mostyn Gibbs as an officer in the Eighth Army, 1942.

The painting is a complex mixture of personal experiences and painterly images. Clearly some of the former were filled out with newspaper reports and pictures of atrocities seen in the summer of 1936. The artist was politically ambivalent about the sides and issues engaged in the war. As the Museum Gallery's director of art, David Alston, puts it, he 'did not indicate his partisanship for one side or the other in the conflict - though obviously for many the Civil War was a defining moment'[97]. Given the intense and many-layered responses made by Cardiff to the Spanish War, it seems fitting that a major artistic record of the event, which faithfully reflects these characteristics, should now be permanently available to its citizens. Between them, Burra's painting and the Welsh International Brigade monument, situated nearby, constitute a delicately-modulated memorial for all sensibilities, a Cardiff poem for Spain.

45.
A Madrid street during the 'siege' by the Nationalists

Appendix 1: International Brigade Volunteers from Cardiff and District (a)

NAME	OCCUPATION	FATE	SOURCE
Body, H.	Seaman	returned ? Oct '38	8
Coles, Bill	Steelworker	killed Jarama Feb '37	1, 4, 8, 9
Cummings, Alec	Ex-soldier	killed Ebro Aug '38	9
Cope, James (b)	Soldier	returned or deserted Jun '37	2
Davies, Harold	?	? returned Oct '38	9
Hamm, Sidney	Student	killed Brunete Jul '37	1, 4, 8, 9
Hyndman, T.A.R.	Ex-soldier	deserted & returned Sept '37	3
Jamadeesis, R. (c)	?	killed details unknown	4, 8
John, Len (d)	?	captured Calaceite Mar '38	5, 9, 13
Jones, Richard (e)	Miner	captured Calaceite Mar '38	10, 11
Levin, M.	?	? returned Oct '38	8, 9
McNulty, Tom	Seaman	? returned Oct '38	8, 9
Morrisey, Bill	Seaman	? returned Oct '38	6, 8, 9, 13
Murphy, Dan	Seaman	killed Gandesa Jul '38	1, 4, 8, 9
Murphy, Pat	Seaman	wounded (twice) & returned Sept '37	1, 5, 8, 9
Nicholls, G.	Railwayman	? returned Oct '38	8, 9
Patterson, Harold	?	wounded Jarama: returned May '37	8, 9, 15

Peters, Robert J.	Plasterer	wounded Brunete: returned Oct '38	12, 13, 14
Price, G.	Miner	? returned Oct '38	8, 9
Stickler, R.	Brass moulder	? returned Oct '38	8, 9
Taylor, Gilbert	Bookshop manager	killed Calaceite Mar '38	1, 7, 8, 9
Taylor, J.	Seaman	killed Ebro Jul '38	8
Traill, Robert	(f)Political activist	killed Brunete Jul '37	1, 4, 8, 9
Stratton, Harry	Taxi driver	returned Oct '37	5, 6
Ward, W.	?	? returned Oct '38	8, 9
Widdess, J.K.	(d)?	c Calaceite Mar '38	5, 8, 9

Notes:

(a) The list includes those who lived in - or had important connections with - the Cardiff area at the time of the Spanish War. Where no other information exists, repatriation with the demobbed Brigades (October 1938) is assumed.

(b) James Arthur Cope of Cardiff was reported by the *Western Mail* on 29th July 1937 as being under detention at Bovingdon (Herts) on a charge of deserting the Royal Tank Corps. He claimed to have been fighting in Spain.

(c) This may possibly be the 'Arab boy' in his mid-teens who went to Spain and was killed, of whom there are still vague memories in Butetown.

(d) H. Francis (source 5) states that these two men were prisoners in San Pedro, but neither name occurs on sources 10 or 11. Since over 200 men on these lists were British, it is strange that only one from Cardiff appears. Lt. Alec Cummings appears on a list of Brigade Staff ('Estado Mayor') dated 7th July in the Salamanca Archive (Seccón Militar, 1061).

(e) Francis states that Jones was from Merthyr Vale, but on two separate occasions (as noted) he recorded his place of residence as Cardiff.

(f) Robert Traill was a Cambridge graduate in languages, who arrived at university from Oundle (Public) School, Northants. He joined the Communist Party as a student and later proceeded to Moscow, enrolling in the Lenin School for training as a

Comintern agent. When the Spanish War broke out he travelled to Republican Spain on a Soviet supply ship. After a period in the Officers' Training School in Valencia he was sent to the Andalusia front as commander of the 20th Battalion in March 1937. Both here and subsequently he distinguished himself in action. Traill was fatally wounded when acting adjutant of the 19th (the second American - 'Washington') Battalion, in the same operation against Villanueva de la Cañada (during the battle of Brunete) in which Pat Murphy too was seriously hurt. Several sources (though with a common root) record him as being from Cardiff, but since it proved impossible to verify this from any fresh evidence, I decided against including Traill's story in the text. Though the evidence from published city directories is inconclusive, it is possible that his parents were living in Cardiff at the time of his birth (i.e. in or around 1914) and left the area when he was still a child. On Traill's background and politics, see A. Sinclair, *The Red and the Blue: Intelligence, Treason and the Universities* (London: Hodder & Stoughton, 1987). On his military record, see J. Monks, *With the Reds in Andalusia* (London: Privately printed, 1986). I found some details about his death in the Archivo Historico Nacional (Civil War Section) in Salamanca: List of Personnel of 19th Battalion, XV International Brigade, 26th June-15th July 1937, Politico Social (Aragón) Legajo 86.

Sources: (for full publication details of books, see Notes)

1. B. Alexander, *British Volunteers for Liberty*
2. *Western Mail*, 29th July 1937.
3. T. Hyndman in P. Toynbee, *The Distant Drum.*
4. Memorial plaque in the South Wales Miners' Library, Swansea (1976).
5. H. Francis, *Miners Against Fascism.*
6. H. Stratton, *To Antifascism by Taxi.*
7. W. Rust, *Britons in Spain*.
8. H. Francis, 'The South Wales Miners and the Spanish Civil War: A Study in Internationalism' (University of Wales Ph.D: Swansea, 1977), Appendix 8.
9. H. Francis, 'List of Welshmen who fought in Spain' (ms., c.1969), in Swansea University Library Archive, S.C. 316.
10. 'Relacion nominal por oficios, nacionalidad y residencia, de los prisioneros extranjeros ingresados en este Campo de Concentracion con fecha 8 del expresado mes a las 2 horas, procedente de Zaragoza', General Army Archive (Avila), Sección Cuartel General del Generalísimo, legajo 56.
11. 'Elenco dei miliziani de nazionalità inglese che si trovano, prigionieri dei nazionali, nel campo di concentramento di San Pedro de Cardena (Burgos)', Foreign Affairs Archive (Madrid), Sección Archivo de Burgos, R-1051, carpeta 75.
12. 'They kept the Red Flag flying': Independent on Sunday, 21st July 1996.
13. Penarth Times, 17th February 1939.
14. Roster of 17th (Lincoln) Battalion, 27th June 1937, National Archive, Seccion Guerra Civil (Salamanca), Politico Social, Aragon, legajo 86.
15. Penarth Times, 6th May 1937.

Appendix 2: Letter from Sid Hamm to Dora Cox, 1937

S.R.I, Playa de Altozano 161
Alboreti, Spain
25th June 1937

Dear Dora,
I have just seen your letter to Jack Williams and was immediately struck with a fit of penitence in which I am scribbling this to you. I don't apologise for not having written before since I hate writing anyhow, & also I thought that Bill Morrisey would keep you informed. Anyway I know you will be pleased to hear that I have put you on my 'once a week' list. The others are Leo Abse, Gerry, mother and now yourself. The others I write to as I get the letters.

You probably know all the news from Jack. We arrived Alboreti 28 April & went straight to Madrigueras. There, for some unknown reason I was made Cultural Leader, a job which now, Thank God (?), I have got rid of. I never did like work anyway. After about 18 days there we proceeded to the front. It was amazing! In the morning we received news that we were leaving for the front at 2 p.m. Immediately all the patients left the hospital, some against doctor's orders, the cooks left the kitchen against orders, the hospital orderlies downed tools & in fact everyone who could hobble or crawl was on parade to go to the front. I've never experienced anything like that before, & believe me was an emotional sensation I shall never forget. Why, about a week after we reached the front a boy we had left in hospital arrived. He had left hospital against orders & tramped & 'hitch-hiked' his way to Jarama, about 70-odd kms.

While we were in Madrigueras we had lectures by Ralph Bates, James Ford, Bob (?Hunter), Cashman, (illegible) & dozens of others such as the Doctor. The most amusing part was the cinema show. First it was silent & like an old time 'Hickie'. It was not continuous & between the reels a 'chairman' got up & made a speech which we all loudly applauded, not knowing what the hell it was about, but 'when in Rome do as the Romans do'. Our other amusements were football, drinking 'cafe leche' (coffee & milk to you) (when we could get it) & buying and eating fruit. Not a very strenuous life you say? That of course we only did during the evening. The morning & afternoon were taken up with route marches, attacks on hills over open country, counterattacks & lectures on military strategy. All this under a blazing sun (quite poetic) we bore willingly, knowing that we were luckier than those who had gone before, in that we got any training. And so, when the time came to fight, we were ready & eager (This tale I will continue in my next. I must keep something to write about).

Jack is down sick here. I don't know what it is, but I hope that it's not serious, although I must say he looks very rough. Anyway the Welsh boys here are looking after him, for he's a great comrade.

I end up on my usual appeal for Players, Chocolate and reading material especially magazines & light novels e.g. Penguins. Well, I'll say au 'vois now, Dora, & will write regularly in future.

Revolutionary greetings to Lewis, Len, John, little John, Gwen, Mrs Aubrey, yourself, etc etc - Sid.

P.S. Bill M(orrisey) is at Madrigueras, Nicholls is in the field telephone (company), Price & Alec Cummings & Pat Murphy here. Bill Coles is dead (more of that later). Find enclosed our paper & some Spanish fags. If you can stand those your TUFF - Sid.

Source: Swansea University Library, S.C. 167.

Notes:

Dora Cox, the recipient of this letter, was at the time serving a sentence in Cardiff jail, imposed for her part in violent incidents during a Blackshirt rally in Tonypandy in 1936.

'James Ford': this is presumably the real owner of the name which is used in Dannie Abse's *Ash on a Young Man's Sleeve* to denote Sid Hamm himself (see p. 116).

'Gwen' is, perhaps, the teacher to whom Bill Coles was engaged (see p. 88).

'Jack' is the Rhondda activist Jack Williams.

The names mentioned in the P.S. suggest that the writer associated them with his political life in Cardiff. This helps to confirm some selective criteria used in assembling the list in Appendix I (see p. 121).

Appendix 3: Archie Cochrane

The story of A.L. Cochrane's service in Spain has been omitted from the main text, on the grounds explained in Appendix 1, note (a). But his subsequent connections with Cardiff and the Valleys are so significant that it would be perverse to exclude it altogether.

Cochrane was born into a wealthy industrialist's family in the Scottish Lowlands in 1909. He was a science student at Cambridge, in much the same generation as Robert Traill, Kim Philby, Julian Bell and other left-wing luminaries who were also to find the call of Spain irresistible. After further study in Vienna - where his hatred of fascism began - he decided on a medical career. In August 1936, he interrupted his training in London to volunteer for the Aid Spain Medical Unit. Cochrane served with tremendous energy for almost a year and his practical influence on the unit was considerable, aside from his being instrumental in its incorporation into the International Brigades. (He is twice 'mentioned in dispatches' in B. Alexander's official history of the British Battalion. His post involved the honorary rank of captain.) He was on duty at a field casualty station all through the battle of Jarama. During the battle of Brunete (July 1937) he was admissions officer for one of the main casualty units situated near the Escorial palace, and must at times have been in charge of Harry Stratton, although neither man knew each other (see p. 106). As a result of the sustained horror of dealing with the wounded and dying of this month-long battle, Cochrane's political disillusionment became acute. Though he had never joined the Party, he now developed a thorough distrust of organised communism. He eventually returned home on pretext of the need to complete his medical training.

Soon after returning from Spain, he became interested in the clinical characteristics of Welsh miners' lung diseases. Though he does not speculate on this in his memoirs, part of his fascination with this problem must surely have been the subliminal political association between the lost cause of the 'worker's struggle' in Spain and the fight against occupational illnesses caused by bad working conditions in the Welsh coalfields. In Wales the cause experienced victory - not, as in Spain, defeat. After the Second World War, around the time of the double triumph of nationalisation in the mining industry and public health, Cochrane came to Cardiff to begin a distinguished career with the Medical Research Council as chief epidemiologist and leading expert in silicosis. For more than thirty years, his base was in Llandough Hospital, which today has a splendid medical library named after him.

In 1941, he was captured during the German invasion of Crete, and endured four years as a prisoner-of-war, acting both as doctor and (since he had good German and Spanish) interpreter. Many of his fellow-prisoners were Spanish republican exiles who had enlisted in the British army of the Near-East in order to continue their struggle against fascism. Whilst in Spain, Cochrane had met both Ernest Hemingway and George Orwell; despite his literary interests, he was impressed with neither. Yet some years later, waiting on Crete for the German parachutists' onslaught, his feelings about Spain came flooding back - so powerfully that he recorded them in the distillation of poetry. It was a delayed-action 'Poem for Spain'.

The branch seemed needle fine
Between me and doom
Of air born death;
But sun on terraced vine
and white, still, broken home
Drew sharp my breath.

I'd been there long before,
When hope was still white bright
For life in Spain.
I'd worked there long before
When heart and mind said 'Fight'
'And die for Spain'.

The issue there was clear;
No shades - only black or white,
Not grey as here.
We knew the fearful stakes,
but doubt was lost in fight,
while here it aches.

....

So friend, remember if you pass this way
To pause and say:
'There is a corner of a Cretan lane
for ever Spain'.[98]

Notes

Only direct quotations are specifically referenced. They are numbered continuously throughout the text. For general acknowledgements, see 'Description of Sources'. Quotations appear exactly as they are printed in source: i.e., no attempt has been made to alter their idiosyncrasies, nor to correct linguistic or factual errors.

Preface

1. Interview with J. Brewer, South Wales Miners' Library, Hendrefoelan, Swansea, transcript JB/57, p. 24.
2. Interview with T. Adlam, Miners' Library, transcript TA/178-9, p. 15.

Chapter One

3. G.A. Williams, 'Imperial South Wales', *The Welsh in Their History* (Beckenham: Croom Helm, 1982), p. 184.
4. H.A. Marquand, 'The Industry and Commerce of Cardiff and District', *The Book of Cardiff: Presented to the Delegates at the Annual Conference of the National Association of Head Teachers* (Oxford: Oxford University Press & London: Humphrey Milford, 1937), p. 84.
5. M.J. Daunton, *Coal Metropolis: Cardiff 1870-1914* (Leicester: Leicester University Press, 1977), p. 66.
6. Williams, 'Imperial South Wales', p. 184.
7. B. Twamley, *Cardiff and Me Fifty Years Ago* (Newport: Starling Press 1980), p. 52.
8. H. Cooke, *How I Saw It: A Str oll Thru' Old Cardiff Bay* (Cardiff: Butetown History & Arts Centre, 1995), p. 45.
9. Twamley, *Cardiff and Me*, p. 76.
10. N.M.C. Sinclair, *The Tiger Bay Story* (Cardiff: Butetown History & Arts Centre, 1993), pp. 51-2.
11. Twamley, *Cardiff and Me*, p. 77.
12. The original Spanish reads:
    'Castilla miserable, ayer dominadora,
    Envuelta en sus harapos desprecia cuanto ignora.'
    A. Machado, *Campos de Castilla*, edited by G. Ribbans (Madrid: Cátedra 1989), p. 103.
13. *The Illtydian* (Midsummer 1938), p. 163.
14. *Western Mail*, 13th May, 1936.
15. Quoted in D. Mitchell, *The Spanish Civil War* (London: Granada, 1982), p. 29. This book is loosely based on the Granada T.V. series of the same name, made in the early 1980s, during which Bebb was interviewed.
16. Quoted in P. Wyden, *The Passionate War: The Narrative History of the Spanish Civil War, 1936-1939* (New York: Simon & Schuster, 1983), p. 39.

Chapter Two

17. P. Lewis, 'The Anglo-Welsh Press response to the Spanish Civil War' (Cardiff: unpublished University of Wales M.A. dissertation, 1990). p. 32.
18. H. Francis, *Miners Against Fascism: Wales and the Spanish Civil War* (London: Lawrence & Wishart, 1984), p. 118.
19. H. Stratton, *To Anti-Fascism by Taxi* (Port Talbot: Alun Books, 1984), pp. 26-7.
20. I. Parrott, *The Spiritual Pilgrims* (Aberystwyth: Christopher Davies, 1969), pp. 134-35.
21. Quoted in T. Buchanan, *The Spanish Civil War and the British Labour Movement* (Cambridge: Cambridge University Press, 1992), p. 82.
22. Quoted in Buchanan, *The Spanish Civil War*, p. 165
23. From Edgell Rickword's 'To the Wife of Any Non-Intervention Statesman', printed in V. Cunningham (ed.), *The Penguin Book of Spanish Civil War Verse* (Harmondsworth: Penguin, 1980), p. 374
24. From unpublished notes on 'A Little Bit of Norway in Wales' (February 1991) made by the witness' son, Prof. J. Greve, copies of which were kindly made available to me by Mr. Allan Milne.
25. *Welsh Catholic Times*, 31st July 1936.
26. *The Universe* (Welsh edition), 21st August 1936.
27. *The Universe* (Welsh edition), 28th August 1936.
28. *Welsh Catholic Times*, 28th August 1936.
29. E.G. Coffey to General Franco, 19th November 1936, Ministry of Foreign Affairs Archive, Madrid (Sección Archivo de Burgos), R-593.
30. *Welsh Catholic Times*, 25th September 1936.
31. *Welsh Catholic Times*, 2nd October, 1936.
32. R. Denning in S. Williams (ed.), *The Cardiff Book* Vol 2 (Barry: Stewart Williams, 1974), p. 53.
33. *Welsh Catholic Times*, 2nd July 1937.
34. *South Wales Echo*, 6th-15th July 1937.
35. *Welsh Catholic Times*, 18th June and 30th July 1937.
36. Archive of the Ministry of Foreign Affairs, Madrid (Seçción Archivo de Burgos) R-1057, document dated 13th April 1938. (Original in Spanish.)
37. J. Fyrth, *The Signal Was Spain: The Spanish Aid Movement in Britain 1936-39* (London: Lawrence and Wishart, 1986), p. 298.
38. *Western Mail*, 25th August 1938. The ensuing correspondence lasted almost a month.
39. *Penarth Times*, 17th February 1939.

Chapter Three

40. *Welsh Catholic Times*, 2nd October 1936.
41. *Hansard*, 3rd December 1936 (5th Series, Vol. 318) col. 1456.
42. *Western Mail*, 19th December 1936.
43. *Western Mail*, 14th July 1937.

44. Reeve-Jones to Foreign Office, 13th July 1937, Public Record Office (Kew), F0 371/21403/13237/41.
45. Note by Under-secretary Shuckburgh, 12th August 1937, Public Record Office (Kew) FO/21403/W15166/13237/41
46. *Western Mail*, 26th July 1937.
47. P. de Azcárate to J. Alvarez del Vayo, 15th October 1937, Archive of Ministry of Foreign Affairs, Madrid (Sección Archivo Renovado), Carpeta R-894/88. (Original in Spanish.)
48. *Western Mail*, 21st October 1937.
49. Quotes from *Western Mail*, 9th March 1938.
50. H. Cooke, *How I Saw It*, p. 7.
51. *South Wales Echo*, 11th August 1937.
52. P.M. Heaton, *Welsh Blockade Runners In the Spanish Civil War* (Newport: Newport: Starling Press, 1985), p. 26.
53. P.M. Heaton, *The Abbey Line:. History of a South Wales Shipping Venture* (Newport: Starling Press, 1983), p. 99.
54. *The Seaman*, 21st December 1938.
55. *Penarth County Girls School Magazine*, Midsummer 1937.
56. Interview included in Granada T.V. Documentary Series 'The Spanish Civil War', made in 1983.
57. Quoted in Heaton, *Welsh Blockade Runners*, p. 45.
58. Quoted in Heaton, *Welsh Blockade Runners*, p. 39.
59. *Western Mail*, 15th July 1937.
60. *South Wales Echo*, 17th July 1937.

Chapter Four

61. Quoted in Heaton, *Welsh Blockade Runners*, pp. 59-61.
62. 'Prisoners of War' by 'Supernumerary' (F. Roberts), *Penarth County School for Girls Magazine* Midsummer 1938, pp. 10-13.
63. H. Shilton to Nationalist Foreign Office, 12th November 1937, Ministry of Foreign Affairs Archive, Madrid (Sección Archivo de Burgos) R-1051/24-110.
64. Quoted (from Robert Browning) in a leaflet issued for Bill Coles Memorial Meeting at Neath Street Hall, Splott, 19th December 1937, Archive of Swansea University, S.C. 214.
65. 'Soldier's Experiences in Spain', *Penarth Times*, 6th May 1937
66. Manuscript account written by P. Murphy for H. Francis (1971), Swansea University Library, S.C. 827.
67. Quoted by M. O'Riordan, *Connolly Column* (New Books: Dublin, 1979), p. 62.
68. *The Seaman*, 9th June 1937.
69. P. Murphy's account, Swansea University Library.
70. Quoted by S. Cronin, *Frank Ryan: The Search for the Republic* (Dublin, 1980), p. 119. Ryan was not present at Brunete, and this story may well have been taken down from Murphy's own lips. At any rate, some of its details seem a little far-fetched.
71. Interview with A. Menai Williams, South Wales Miners' Library, transcript AMW/

2/7.

72. *Western Mail*, 7th November 1936.

73. F.H. Thomas, 'Spanish Legionario: A Professional Soldier in Spain' (unpublished typescript memoirs, 1938), p. 60.

74. E. Lister, *Memorias de un luchador* Vol. I (Madrid: Editorial Toro, 1977), pp. 223-24. (Original in Spanish.)

75. Thomas, 'Spanish Legionario', pp. 33-4.

76. Thomas, 'Spanish Legionario', pp. 77-8.

77. 'I may say that I loathe ...'

Quoted in W. Rust, *Britons in Spain* (London: Lawrence & Wishart, 1939) p. 130.

78. From W. Morrisey's letters to Edward Thomas (Newport), Swansea University Library, S.C. 606-14.

79. *Penarth Times*, 17th February 1939.

80. Quoted from an interview published in 'They kept the Red Flag flying', by Brian Cathcart and Isambard Wilkinson, *Independent on Sunday*, 21st July 1996.

81. S. Spender, *World Within World* (London: Faber & Faber, 1977), p. 184.

82. T.A.R. Hyndman, 'International Brigader 2' in P. Toynbee (ed.), *The Distant Drum: Reflections on the Spanish Civil War* (London: Book Club edn., 1976), pp. 122-23.

83. Quoted in Spender, *World Within World*, p. 213.

84. Quoted in Spender, *World Within World*, pp. 213-14.

85. T.C. Worsley, *Behind the Battle* (London: Robert Hale, 1939), pp. 259-60.

86. Spender, *World Within World*, p. 228.

87. Hyndman in Toynbee, *The Distant Drum*, p. 128.

88. Quoted in M. Shipton, 'Top poet saved gay lover from the firing squad' *Wales on Sunday*, November 19th 1995.

89. Printed in V. Cunningham (ed.), *Penguin Book of Spanish Civil War Verse*, p. 193. The poem was originally published in *Poems for Spain* (London: Faber & Faber, 1939) edited by Spender and John Lehmann. A Spanish translation has appeared in R. Alvarez Rodríguez & R. López Ortega (eds.), *Poesia Anglo-Norteamericana de la Guerra Civil Española: antologia bilingüe* (Salamnca, 1986) p.111.

90. D. Abse, 'My First Book', in *The Author* (Spring 1996), p. 16. (I am grateful to Dr. Abse for letting me have a copy of this item.)

91. D. Abse, *Ash On A Young Man's Sleeve*, (London: Vallentine, Mitchell, 3rd edn. 1971), pp. 74-8. (I am grateful to Dr. Abse's agents, Sheil Land Associates, for permission to quote from work.)

92. Memorial Pamphlet published by Cardiff United Youth Movement (1937), Swansea University Library, S.C. 177.

93. Abse, *Ash On A Young Man's Sleeve* p. 75.

94. D. Abse, *A Poet in the Family* (London: Robson Books, 1984), p. 6.

95. Printed in *The Illtydian* (Easter 1937).

96. D. Abse, 'My First Book', p. 16.

97. Leaflet by D. Alston, Keeper of Art, produced to mark the inaugural showing of Burra's painting at the Welsh National Museum Gallery in November, 1995.

Appendix 3

98. A.L. Cochrane with M. Blythe, *One Man's Medicine: An autobiography of Professor Archie Cochrane* (London: The Memoir Club & British Medical Journal, 1989), p. 52. Cochrane's contribution to the saving of lives in Spain is also referred to several times in Fyrth, *The Signal Was Spain*, between pp. 43-94.

Description of Sources

What follows provides details about the sources on which the text has been based, amplifying skeletal references in the chapter-notes, for the benefit of readers who wish to pursue matters of interest.

1. Primary Sources

a) Unpublished Documentary Materials

Archive of the Ministry of Foreign Affairs, Madrid:

- Records of the Republican and Nationalist Foreign Offices.

General Military Archive, Avila

- Records of the military administration of nationalist Spain and captured republican documents (ditto).

Archive of the British International Brigade Association, Marx Memorial Library, London:

- A varied collection of records concerning British involvement in the Spanish War

British Library, Newspaper Section, Colindale, London - (see below)

Glamorgan County Archives, Cardiff:

- Press cuttings from Cardiff City Police files

Public Record Office, Kew:

- State Papers of British Central Government Departments

Spanish National Historic Archive (Civil War Section, Salamanca):

- Administrative Records of the International Brigades (incomplete)

Swansea Miners' Library, Hendrefoelan (see below):

- Also has a varied collection of printed and photographic materials concerning Wales' involvement in the Spanish War

South Wales Coalfield Library, University of Swansea:

- Material relating to the Spanish Civl War, including letters from International Brigaders (Section 60, S.C.)

'Spanish Legionario: A Professional Soldier in Spain' by F.H. Thomas (in private possession)

b) Interviews

i. Conducted by the author in connection with the present work.

Subjects: Luis Cicero, Mary Cicero, Harry Cooke, Sissie Davidson, Vera Drakakis,

Alun Emlyn-Jones, Joan Evans, Christopher Hill, Jean Howells, Joe Larreta, Dan O'Neill, Doris Perez, Robert Peters, Norrie Russ, Frank Sanchez, Nancy Smith.

ii. Conducted by Hywel Francis and others in connection with research on the Welsh International Brigaders: transcripts kept in the South Wales Miners' Library. Subjects: Tom Adlam, Jim Brewer, Mike O'Donoghue, Leo Price, Lance Rogers, Alun Menai Williams.

c) Newspapers and Magazines
The following were consulted at the British Library, Colindale; Penarth Public Library; Cardiff Central Library; South Wales Miners' Library; and Glamorgan County Archives. *The Illtydian, The Penarth Times, The Seaman, The South W ales Echo, The Universe, The Welsh Catholic Times, The Western Mail.*

2. Bibliographical Essay
N.B. With only a few exceptions, I have not included publications available only in Spanish.

A brief illustrated introduction to Spanish History, from the earliest times to the present day, can be found in M. Vincent & R. Stradling, *A Cultural Atlas of Spain and Portugal* (New York: Facts on File, 1994). The most comprehensive and reliable one-volume study of *The Spanish Civil War* in any language is that of H. Thomas (Harmondsworth: Penguin, 2nd edition, 1977). More digestible introductions to the topic are available, including illustrated paperbacks by P. Preston, *A Concise History of the Spanish Civil War* (London: Fontana-Collins, 1996), and D. Mitchell, *The Spanish Civil War* (London: Granada, 1982). Also useful is S. Ellwood's booklet, *The Spanish Civil War* (Oxford: Blackwell paperback, 1993), though it lacks illustrations. M. Alpert, *A New International History of the Spanish Civil War* (London: Macmillan, 1994) offers a treatment of the blockade of Bilbao and other maritime aspects of the war, based on the author's own earlier monograph, available only in Spanish.

H. Francis' scholarly and readable study of *Miners Against Fascism: Wales and the Spanish Civil War* (London: Lawrence & Wishart, 1984) is indispensable for a full understanding of the context of Cardiff's (or any other Welsh locality's) response to the Spanish War. In its original dissertation form, 'The Welsh Miners and the Spanish Civil War: A Study in Internationalism' (University Library, Swansea), the work has a second volume of useful data. M. Daunton, *Coal Metropolis: Cardiff 1870-1914* (Leicester: Leicester University Press, 1977) is essential on the creation of modern Cardiff, but W. Rees, *History of Cardiff* (Cardiff: Corporation of Cardiff, 1962 edn.) is still important for a deeper perspective. An 'official' overview is given in G. Dart (et al.), *Cardiff 1889-1974: The Story of a County Borough* (Cardiff: Corporation of Cardiff, 1994). J. Hickey's monograph, *Urban Catholics: Urban Catholicism in England and Wales from 1829 to the present day* (London: The Catholic Book Club, 1967) is based on rich statistical material about the living conditions of Irish immigrants in Cardiff. Idiomatic stories of life in the Docklands are related by B. Twamley, *Cardiff and Me Fifty Years Ago* (Newport: Starling Press, 1980) and H. 'Shipmate' Cooke, *How I Saw It: A Str oll Thru' Old Cardiff* (Cardiff: Butetown History & Arts Centre, 1995) - the former more moving, the latter enlivened by poetry and illustration. Details of the monument in Cathays Park can be found in C. Williams & J. Gorman, *Memorials of the Spanish Civil War* (Stroud: Alan Sutton, 1996). P. Stead's useful survey of inter-war Barry, 'The Town that had Come of Age, 1918-1938' can be found in D. Moore (ed.), *Barry: The Centenary Book* (Barry: Barry Town Council, 1984). The various works of T.M. Heaton represent an indispensable record of the South Wales shipping industry. In the present book I have used his *Welsh Blockade Runners in the Spanish Civil War* (Newport, 1985) and *The Abbey Line: History of a South Wales Shipping Venture* (Newport, 1983), both published by Starling Press. On the Basque Country, I have supplemented my personal experience with *Pais Vasco* (Bilbao: El Pueblo Vasco, 1994), a magnificently illustrated survey by many hands, co-ordinated by M. Montero.

T. Buchanan, *The Spanish Civil War and the British Labour Movement* (Cambridge: Cambridge University Press, 1992) critically analyzes the labour movement's response to the war. I have used this in conjunction with J. Fyrth,. *The Signal Was Spain: The Spanish Aid Movement in Britain, 1936-39* (London: Lawrence & Wishart, 1986). General information about Catholic reactions to Fascism can be gleaned from D.S. Lewis, *Illusions of Grandeur: Mosley, Fascism and British Society, 1931-81* (Manchester: Manchester University Press, 1984) and the essay by S. Rawnsley, 'The Membership of the B.U.F.' in K. Lunn and R. Thurlow (eds.), *British Fascism: Essays on the Radical Right in Inter-War Britain* (London: Croom Helm, 1980). A sustained investigation of the most dramatic and influential incident in the Spanish War, is H. Southworth, *Guernica! Guernica! A Study of Journalism, Diplomacy, Propaganda and History* (Berkeley: University of California Press, 1977). Equally committed is B. Alexander's official history of the British Brigaders, *British Volunteers for Liberty: Spain, 1936-39* (London: Lawrence and Wishart, 1986). A general survey, much less sympathetic to the party line, is R.D. Richardson, *Comintern Army: The International Brigades and the Spanish Civil War* (Lexington: University of Kentucky Press, 1982).

Other uncited works include H. David, *Stephen Spender - A Life* (London: Heinemann, 1992); L. Bartlett (ed.), *Letters to Christopher* (Santa Barbara: California University Press, 1980); J. Goldsmith (ed.), *Spender's Journals, 1939-83* (London: Faber & Faber, 1985). Also on T.A.R. Hyndman, see D. O'Neill's feature article 'Tom's Days of Sunshine and Despair: A Cardiff Footnote to the Spanish Civil War', in the *South Wales Echo*, 2nd August 1976. B. Griffiths, *Saunders Lewis* (Cardiff: University of Wales Press, 1979), is useful but carefully elides its subject's attitudes to the continental dictators. For a detailed study of the nationalist offensives aimed at capturing Madrid in 1936-37, see G. Hills, *The Battle for Madrid* (London: Vantage, 1976). The relative absence of terror in the Basque zone is well illustrated in C. Crespo Nogueira, *Justicia en Guerra. Jornada sobre la Administración de Justicia durante la Guerra de Espana; Institutiones y Fuentes Documentales* (Madrid: Ministerio de Cultura, 1990). For the Irish part in the Spanish War, see my illustrated feature on 'Franco's Irish Volunteers' in the magazine *History Today* for April, 1995; and my essay 'Battleground of Reputations: Ireland and the Spanish Civil War' in P. Preston & A. Mackenzie (eds.), *The Republic Besieged: Civil War in Spain, 1936-1939* (Edinburgh: Edinburgh University Press, 1996)

Picture Acknowledgements

(NB In spite every effort, it proved impossible to contact some of the listed sources, to whom apologies are offered for any infringement.)

South Wales Echo & Western Mail 2, 15, 17, 18, 39, 41; The Independent on Sunday 37; Toronto Daily Star 33; D. Abse 42; Stewart Williams Publications 3, 4, 5, 10; N Gibbs 44; A Emlyn Jones 14, 20; A Carter 22, 27; J Larreta 26, 29; L Cicero 25; R J Peters 35, 36; N Smith 31; P Perez 7; Granada Publications 21, 24; Harry Stratton 38; Weidefeld & Nicholson 9, 40, 45; Barrie & Rockcliff, London 16; Penguin Books 8; H Stradling 30, 34; R Stradling 32; Ministry of Foreign Affairs, Madrid 28; Servicio Historico Militar, Avila 23; South Wales Coalfield Collection, University of Swansea Library 6, 11, 12, 13, 43; Derek Williams Collection, National Museum and Gallery, Cardiff 1; Simon & Schuster 23; Butetown History & Arts Centre 19.

Index